UNIVERSITY OF CAMBRIDGE
DEPARTMENT OF APPLIED ECONOMICS

MONOGRAPHS

3

THE ROLE OF MEASUREMENT
IN ECONOMICS

THE
ROLE OF MEASUREMENT
IN ECONOMICS

BY

RICHARD STONE

DIRECTOR OF THE DEPARTMENT OF APPLIED ECONOMICS
FELLOW OF KING'S COLLEGE, CAMBRIDGE

THE NEWMARCH LECTURES
1948–1949
given at University College, London

CAMBRIDGE
AT THE UNIVERSITY PRESS
1951

CAMBRIDGE UNIVERSITY PRESS
Cambridge, New York, Melbourne, Madrid, Cape Town,
Singapore, São Paulo, Delhi, Mexico City

Cambridge University Press
The Edinburgh Building, Cambridge CB2 8RU, UK

Published in the United States of America by Cambridge University Press, New York

www.cambridge.org
Information on this title: www.cambridge.org/9781107673861

© Cambridge University Press 1951

First published 1951
First paperback edition 2013

A catalogue record for this publication is available from the British Library

ISBN 978-1-107-67386-1 Paperback

CONTENTS

vi CONTENTS

LIST OF TABLES

LIST OF DIAGRAMS

PREFACE

It was my privilege to give the Newmarch Lectures for the academic year 1948–9 at University College, London. In preparing them for publication I have thought it best to leave the topics in their original order, but not to divide the text of this essay into four sections corresponding to the individual lectures. The ground covered by each of these is contained in Sections I–VI, VII–XIII, XIV–XXI, and XXII–XXIX respectively, and the only extensions I have made are as follows. The topics of Sections VI and X were barely touched upon in the lectures themselves and are expanded here. The numerical illustration of Section XVI has been revised in the light of the national income White Paper which appeared in April 1949 and a detailed explanation of the way in which these figures have been derived has been added. Time did not permit any reference to the details of Section XVII or to the studies described in Sections XXVII and XXVIII.

I am indebted to two members of the Department of Applied Economics for the help they have given in preparing this book for publication. Section VI has benefited from the criticisms of Mr J. Durbin and I was assisted in the presentation of Section X by Mr S. F. James.

The temerity of attempting to cover so large a subject in so small a space is obvious. For the benefit of any who may wish to pursue the various topics further I have included a number of references, mostly to the literature of the last decade. The list is in no sense comprehensive; it contains simply those books and articles which have seemed to me most relevant among those I happen to have come across.

J.R.N.S.

CAMBRIDGE

August 1949

INTRODUCTION

I. NEWMARCH AND THE PROGRESS OF
STATISTICAL INQUIRY

William Newmarch, whom we remember and honour in these lectures, will be known to all of you as a great economic statistician. Born in Yorkshire in 1820, he made his career in insurance and finance. As a young man he came to live in London and in his leisure hours devoted much of his immense energies to furthering the science of statistics. He was especially active in the Statistical Society of London (as the Royal Statistical Society then was) and contributed some eighteen papers and communications to its *Journal*, which he edited for many years. He was a Liberal, for many years a leading member of the Reform Club, a Fellow of the Royal Society and an active member of the Political Economy Club. He collaborated with Tooke in the two final volumes of Tooke's *History of Prices* and was responsible for a great part of the work of these volumes. In 1863 he started the Annual Commercial History in *The Economist*. He died in 1882.

In the session of 1869–70 he succeeded Mr Gladstone as President of the Statistical Society and devoted his inaugural address to the Progress and Present Condition of Statistical Inquiry.* If we look back at the course of statistical inquiry over the last eighty years it is remarkable how clearly Newmarch saw many of the subjects which would engage the attention of economic statisticians in succeeding generations. He lists the eighteen fields of research most requiring early attention, of which the first four are:

(1) The annual consumption per head among different classes, and by the nation as a whole, of the chief articles of food—corn, butchers' meat, tea, coffee, sugar, tobacco, wine, spirits and beer.

(2) The annual production in agriculture, minerals, metals, ships and manufactures.

(3) The comparative wages, house-rent, and cost of living in different parts of the country.

(4) The total annual income and earnings and the total annual accumulations of different classes, and of the country as a whole.

While I am tempted to digress on these topics it is really the last item in the list which I shall take as the text for these lectures. Newmarch described it thus:

(18) Investigations of the mathematics and logic of Statistical Evidence; that is to say, the true construction and use of Averages, the deduction of probabilities, the exclusion of superfluous integers, and the discovery of the laws of such social phenomena as can only be exhibited by a numerical notation.

* See *Journal of the Statistical Society of London*, vol. XXXII, pt. IV (December 1869), pp. 359–90.

In commenting on this topic he remarks that it

relates to the mathematics and logic of Statistics, and therefore, as many will
think, to the most fundamental inquiry with which we can be occupied....
This abstract portion of the inquiries we cultivate is still, however, in the first
stages of growth. It is certain that by means of the averages, and variations
of increase and decrease, presented by large masses of figures representing
social phenomena which occur within longer or shorter intervals of time and
within defined limits, it is possible to arrive at conclusions which so far
resemble the law of the several cases that they justify the enunciation of
probabilities and predictions.

At the time when Newmarch uttered these words the study of
economics differed in many respects from its position to-day. On the
factual side huge masses of statistical data were being collated and
interpreted by such writers as Porter,* Tooke † and Newmarch himself.
Comparatively little had been done to work up this material into
the empirical correlates of the concepts used in economic theories,
though Baxter's remarkable book ‡ on the national income had recently
appeared. On the theoretical side the mathematical expression of
economic relationships, essential if a quantitative analysis is to be
attempted, was in its infancy. Cournot had published his great
Recherches § a generation earlier, but the works of Jevons‖ and Léon
Walras ¶ were only on the eve of their appearance. Mathematical
economics was hardly known, let alone established, and that combination of theoretical and empirical studies which has flourished in recent
years under the name of econometrics was for all practical purposes
unheard of. As time went on more and more facts of a quantitative
kind about the economic situation came to be collected and published
while economic theory grew rapidly. At the end of the nineteenth
century Marshall, addressing an undergraduate audience at Cambridge,
could say:** 'Speaking generally the nineteenth century has in great
measure achieved *qualitative* analysis in economics; but it has not gone
farther. It has felt the necessity of *quantitative* analysis, and has made
some rough preliminary surveys of the way in which it is to be achieved:
but the achievement itself stands over for you.'

In recent years these two different approaches to economic problems,
the factual and the theoretical, have been brought much closer together.
In attempting to give quantitative expression to empirical constructs,
such as the national income, it is now generally recognized that a

* *The Progress of the Nation* (1st edit. 1836–8), by G. R. Porter.
† *A History of Prices* (6 vols.), by T. Tooke assisted in the last two volumes by
W. Newmarch.
‡ *The National Income* (1868), by D. Baxter.
§ *Recherches sur les Principes Mathématiques de la Théorie des Richesses* (1839), by
A. A. Cournot. An English edition appeared in 1897.
‖ *The Theory of Political Economy* (1871), by W. S. Jevons.
¶ *Eléments d'Economie Politique Pure* (1874), by L. Walras.
** 'The Old Generation of Economists and the New', by A. Marshall, in *Quarterly
Journal of Economics* (January 1897).

theoretical basis is necessary and that this basis should be the conscious concern of economists and not left in its practical aspect exclusively to business men, accountants and the Commissioners of Inland Revenue. Equally is it clear that economic theory cannot usefully be left at the theoretical stage but requires to be tested and given quantitative expression by being brought into relation with observations. These lines of attack have resulted in very considerable efforts to bring into being both observations which are relevant to economic theories, and also theories, or formulations of theories, which are capable of being brought into relation with observations.

One important result of these developments has been a growing cleavage among economists. This cleavage has not been along political lines, which when it occurs is doubtless unavoidable, nor even along doctrinal lines, in the sense of opposing explanations of the same phenomena, but along technical lines. The econometric approach with its inevitable emphasis on mathematics in formulating theories and analysing observations calls for a technical knowledge if its methods are to be understood, let alone used, which many economists and economic statisticians do not possess and do not see the need of. There is a reluctance to believe that the complexities of economic change can ever be ensnared in a mathematical net, or rather there is a misunderstanding of the part which the mathematical net must play in getting the economic fish to the table. This stage of the debate can conveniently be summarized in the words of Lord Keynes in his final comment in the celebrated discussion over Tinbergen's League of Nations studies:*

No one could be more frank, more painstaking, more free from subjective bias or *parti pris* than Professor Tinbergen. There is no one, therefore, so far as human qualities go, whom it would be safer to trust with black magic. That there is anyone I would trust with it at the present stage or that this brand of statistical alchemy is ripe to become a branch of science, I am not yet persuaded. But Newton, Boyle and Locke all played with alchemy. So let him continue.

There was certainly much to criticize in early attempts at econometrics with its crudeness and over-optimism; its promise, unlike its performance, was unlimited. But after the first flush of stupendous enthusiasm econometricians have settled down to the job of improving their tools for the task of analysing and predicting economic change. We have still a long way to go, but the change in outlook is unmistakable and should help to heal the division among contemporary economists that I have just mentioned. Let me give some examples of this.

A great deal of econometric work has been devoted to building and testing models, that is systems of relationships designed to show the interdependent variation of a set of variables, and with estimating the constants or parameters in these models. It has been common practice

* 'Statistical Business-Cycle Research: Comment', by J. M. Keynes, in *The Economic Journal*, vol. L (March 1940), pp. 154–6.

to write the relationships in the form of linear multivariate regression equations and to pay comparatively little attention to the fact that they are not exact. They have never of course been regarded as exact by the investigators who have used them, but they are sometimes expressed in a form which may possess a misleading and repellant air of certainty to sceptical observers. Moreover, a system of equations in which the values of some variables appear for consecutive time periods can be used for prediction purposes, but the predictions which can be derived express the way in which the system would vary through time if it were allowed to run undisturbed, that is as if the whole story had been reproduced in the equations. Obviously, however, it has not, for the equations are known to be inexact even during the observation period over which the parameters are determined. The effect of these shocks or disturbances which we have not been able to ensnare in the mathematical net is that in practice the system may very well develop quite differently from the prediction based on the systematic part of the relationships. If we can say something about the dispersion of the shocks we can say something about the margin of error of the predictions, granted that the systematic part of the model can be assumed to apply to the future. If the system is stationary there will be an upper limit to these margins of error, but if it is of a wandering type, which may be the case in practice, the margins will grow without limit, though this is only likely to be important in very long-term predictions.

This aspect of the matter is now explicitly recognized and great care is taken to specify the assumed properties of the disturbances since they have an important bearing not only on prediction but also on the estimation of parameters. But while attention to the disturbances will help us to make better models and will make us more aware of their limitations for purposes of prediction there is a limit beyond which it will not help us to make better predictions. We know that in each future period a variable we are studying will be shifted a bit off its course, as otherwise determined, by a disturbance whose mean effect we can estimate but whose actual effect in any particular instance is unknown. Any guidance as to the specific direction and magnitude of a future shock is something which we can only obtain from a knowledge of affairs and a capacity to see which way things are going combined with an understanding of the model. To deny this is equivalent to saying that we can construct exact models, which nobody believes. Thus the roles of the econometrician and the practical economist are complementary rather than antagonistic when viewed in their true light. The econometrician's role is to provide information about the systematic factors at work so that the inevitable element of guess-work is reduced as far as possible. All practical economists who are not econometricians will readily assent to this statement in so far as it relates to identities or definitions. No one in his senses will be content with predictions of income, outlay, saving, etc., which do not satisfy the usual accounting identities. But these identities are only useful because they set limits to the possible joint variation of a set of variables. Behaviouristic and institutional relationships play an exactly similar part. Given a set of disturbed or stochastic equations the practical economist has to guess the effect of the play in the system and not the whole of its variation.

But, you may say, there is surely something to be said for the view just attributed to the practical economist. Surely behaviouristic relations have not the permanence and universality of definitions. No doubt; but the question is one of fact, and investigations, e.g. into market demand and the consumption function, show that many behaviouristic relationships have in practice a very considerable permanence. The point I want to make is that in the econometric literature of the present time this question of the permanence of relationships is being closely investigated and the necessity for dealing with breaks in structure, as they are called, is fully recognized.

These examples of recent trends in econometric work should help, I think, to re-establish a belief in the reasonableness of what econometricians are trying to do among economists whose approach is different. In my view econometrics is an essential part of applied economics and one which on the whole has been sadly neglected in this country. Its intellectual position must be accepted by all who believe that there is a considerable measure of regularity and system in economic life.

II. ECONOMICS AND MEASUREMENT

As I am going to talk about the part played by measurement in economics I propose at this point to say a little about these terms. The essentially economic aspect of a problem has been defined by Professor Robbins in saying that 'economics is the science which studies human behaviour as a relationship between ends and scarce means which have alternative uses'.* This way of putting the matter brings out the important point that, while many situations in actual life have an economic aspect, few if any can be analysed wholly in economic terms. Taken literally, however, it would bring the applied economist practically to a full stop since he cannot in general estimate the importance of economic factors unless he is prepared to make assumptions about, and if necessary arrange to hold roughly constant, certain non-economic factors such as changes in tastes. In fact he can frequently do this for himself in a rough-and-ready way although undoubtedly it would be a gain if he could fall back on other branches of the social sciences for help in such matters. The moral of Robbins's definition is that in applied work much more integration of the social sciences is needed.

Measurement is concerned with finding an expression for the degree of difference in distinguishable qualities or characteristics. It is possible if a means can be found for bringing the amount of any characteristic

* See *An Essay on the Nature and Significance of Economic Science* (2nd edit. 1936), by L. C. Robbins, p. 15.

under investigation into a certain relationship with a set of numbers.*
Thus we may bring the weight of pig-iron produced at different blast
furnaces into relation with a set of numbers and express the different
outputs as so many tons in each case. But evidently there is no need for
the set of numbers to be unique; for in the above instance, by a mere
change of unit, we should obtain a new set of numbers, e.g. if we expressed the result in pounds or in kilograms. But all these different sets
of numbers can be obtained from one another by multiplication by
a constant; for example if y is the weight expressed in pounds and x is
the weight expressed in tons then $y = 2240x$ and so on. Different
measures obtained from one another by multiplication by a constant
are related by a straight line relationship which passes through the
zero-point on the scale of each measure simultaneously. In mathematical language we may speak of one measure being obtained from
another by means of a linear transformation through the origin. In
such circumstances it is unambiguous to say that in one case there is
twice as much of a characteristic as in another since if this is shown by
one measure it will also be shown by any member of the infinite set of
alternative measures obtained by multiplication by constants.

In some cases it will not be possible to derive alternative measures
from one another in this simple way. Consider for example the three
scales commonly used in measuring the degree of heat—Centigrade,
Réaumur and Fahrenheit. Denoting these respectively by C, R and F,
it is well known that C and R are derived from one another by multiplication by a constant. In fact

$$R = 0.8C.$$

But this is not true of the relationship of F and C. For

$$F = 32 + 1.8C.$$

Here the transformation is linear but does not go through the origin.

In economics it is frequently necessary to adopt measures, for example
measures of the general level of prices or production, which are not
unique and cannot be obtained from alternative similar measures by
linear transformations through the origin. Such measures usually take
the form of index numbers. Let us concentrate on a quantity index
number of the most familiar kind, namely the base-weighted aggregative
usually written in the form $\Sigma p_0 q_1 / \Sigma p_0 q_0$. This expression means that we
revalue the quantities of period 1 at the prices of period 0, add the values
obtained together and divide by the sum of the values in period 0. Now,
if all the indicators, the q's, vary in proportion then the index will
obviously show the same proportionate movements whatever set of
weights, the p_0's, we choose to take. But suppose that while each indicator is perfectly correlated with every other one they do not all vary in

* For a rigorous statement of the formal conditions of measurement see *An Introduction to Logic and Scientific Method* (abridged edit. 1939), by M. R. Cohen and E. Nagel,
pp. 187–8.

proportion. In this case it is not difficult to see that by taking different weights we shall get different index numbers which cannot be obtained from one another by multiplication by constants. In fact the relationship will be linear but it will not pass through the origin. In such a case the statement, that the characteristic measured by the index has doubled, is ambiguous; we must know what weights have been used. As we relax the restriction on the correlation between the indicators so we shall pass further away from the position in which alternative index numbers using different weights are simply related to one another.

Now if, in making index numbers, we were free to take any set of weights and if the indicators were not at all closely related it is clear that the measures represented by the index numbers would be quite useless. But in fact neither of these conditions is normally met with. We usually find a considerable degree of correlation between indicators and also between the different sets of weights that we should ever think of using. Consequently we are likely to find that alternative index numbers using different weights show similar and often approximately proportionate movements. That this is so in most economic applications is due to the nature of the actual world and not simply to the formal characteristics of index-number techniques.

In talking of index numbers I have taken a case where we propose a method of measurement and then ask whether in practice the results to be obtained are likely to possess the characteristics normally associated with measurement. The question of measurability may, however, arise as a theoretical issue. For example the measurability of utility has for long been in debate. If the relationships of preference and indifference have certain formal properties—and whether they do or do not is a matter of fact—then it can be shown that utility is measurable.* On the usually accepted postulates about the two relationships, however, utility is not measurable but can be ordered. So far from alternative measures being related by linear transformations through the origin, they are related by arbitrary monotonic transformations. Thus the measurability of different characteristics can be brought into the same universe of discourse by considering the generality of permitted transformations of scale.

III. FOUR TYPES OF QUESTION IN ECONOMICS

With this somewhat lengthy introduction I shall now set out briefly the way I propose to treat the role of measurement in economics in these lectures. I shall divide the questions which have to be answered, in attempting to obtain and apply economic knowledge, into four classes. The first class comprises questions of fact, and includes empirical constructs such as the income of an individual or a nation and the level of

* See 'Über die Messbarkeit des Nutzens', by F. Alt, in *Zeitschrift für National-ökonomie*, vol. VII (1936), pp. 161–9, and *Theory of Games and Economic Behavior* (2nd edit. 1947), by J. von Neumann and O. Morgenstern, ch. I, sect. 3 and appendix.

retail prices. The second comprises questions of the truth or falsity of an hypothesis or theory such as whether or not the relationship of preference is transitive or whether or not the Keynesian theory is able to account for certain observed events. The third comprises questions of the estimation of parameters. This will in many cases mean the estimation of the extent to which a change in one variable affects another, for example the extent to which a change in the price of beer will, other things being equal, affect consumption. The final class comprises questions of prediction. These may be of a conditional nature, such as the question: What will be the level of the national income next year given the level next year of asset formation and government expenditure? or unconditional, such as the question: What will be the price of bricks in five years' time?

FOUR ASPECTS OF THE PROBLEM OF MEASUREMENT

IV. FACTS AND EMPIRICAL CONSTRUCTS

It is obvious that there is an enormous amount of descriptive material, sometimes called natural history data, about economic activity in all its forms. A great deal of this will not involve measurement at all, since it will consist of descriptions of the organization and working of institutions and agreements and arrangements of all kinds. In addition to this qualitative descriptive material there is a vast mass of quantitative descriptive material. Part of the latter arises from the labours of book-keepers, clerks and others engaged in recording, classifying and presenting records of some form of activity. This part of the quantitative descriptive material normally relates to the records of a single organization or concern, though this may of course be very large and have many branches. Another part arises from an attempt to collect information from a number of separate units as exemplified by the greater part of official statistics. Classified and tabulated information of this kind contributes to the body of knowledge known as economic statistics.

In addition to this body of descriptive material, consisting of what I propose to call primary facts, there is on the quantitative side a further type of information which may be called empirical constructs. It may be that from a philosophical point of view these constructs are not to be sharply differentiated from primary facts and that the difference, if any, is only one of degree. By primary facts I mean such things as the originating entries in a cash book or the quantity of some commodity produced over a particular period. It is not as a rule hard to find a definition for items of this kind and the problem of obtaining information about them lies largely in the administrative and technical difficulties of collection. On the other hand there are many items, similar to primary facts in having a counterpart in the actual world, but which are not capable of being apprehended in the same simple manner. These empirical constructs are well illustrated by the example of the income of an individual or a nation. No amount of searching in primary records, that is the originating entries, actual or imputed, in the books of a firm or individual, will enable us to detect the income that has been made. To ascertain income it is necessary to set up a theory from which income is derived as a concept by postulation and then associate this concept with a certain set of primary facts. To be sure the theory must take into account possible primary facts if it is to be of any practical use since if it does not the theoretical concept of income will be left hanging in the air, with no empirical correlate. But some theory is necessary since without it income does not reveal itself in the simple way as do the individuals and pieces of equipment which are largely responsible for generating it.

The principal problems which the answering of questions of fact sets to the economic statistician can conveniently be analysed in the familiar terms of demand and supply. We first have to decide what we want to know and then consider how we are going to find it out. From the point of view of the user of factual information the obvious approach to the first question is to specify first what he wants to know and how accurately he wants to know it, and then arrange for it to be collected. A system for ascertaining facts which worked on this principle I shall describe as one which embodies, potentially at least, the maximum amount of *economic design*, since I am assuming that the economic facts that would be wanted would have been carefully defined in the light of the theoretical principles that were to be used in interpreting and relating them. It will come as no surprise to anyone with the smallest acquaintance with economic statistics to be told that this is not how most economic facts are ascertained. In practice one does not as a rule have the information one wants but something rather different, with the consequence that tedious and uncertain adjustments, if not wholesale guesswork, must be made in order to estimate what is required. This state of affairs is such a commonplace that it comes in for far less criticism than it deserves.

Let us now look at the supply side of the picture. The problem here is to collect and present the required information at minimum cost subject to the proviso that it comes up to the prescribed level of accuracy. There is no point in trying to ascertain the national income on some given definition to the nearest £ when in fact no use for the information could be conceived that required it to be accurate to more than the nearest £10 million. On the other hand it is very desirable to know how accurate such estimates are since otherwise an error of observation may be mistaken for an actual change. Also it is important to distinguish and if possible to eliminate sources of systematic error, or bias, or at least to reduce such errors to well within the prescribed tolerance. A system for ascertaining facts which worked on this basis I shall describe as one which embodies the maximum of *statistical design*. This property is not possessed in any high degree by most of the arrangements which exist at present for collecting economic statistics.

The reasons are clear why there is so little either of economic or of statistical design in the official statistics on which economists must largely depend. Economic information, like anything else, is produced in response to effective demand. Much of the information that has become necessary in the last decade for new administrative purposes has been wanted by economists for a much longer time but the demand has only recently become effective. The magnitude of this change can hardly be exaggerated and the present level of effective demand for economic statistics would, I think, persist under any form of government that is likely to be put in office. At the same time this great increase in the demand for quantitative economic information has not suddenly arisen from nothing at all. Particular administrative needs have for many years resulted in information being provided to meet those needs or as a by-product of administration, as in the case of the information provided by the Commissioners for Inland Revenue or through the working of the Unemployment Insurance Acts.

Now if we look at the matter from the point of view of this older type of administrative need such as was predominant before the war it will be evident that a number of factors conspire to prevent the emphasis on economic and statistical design. The very fact that information on, say, income or consumption is derived as a by-product of some administrative process means that the particular definitions adopted for that administrative process will be reflected in the statistics. It is not to be expected that such definitions will be easily changed or even always can be changed to suit a wider purpose and the fact that such information does exist will cause reluctance to undertake further collections which to the layman will seem scarcely different. Furthermore, for many administrative purposes, action on each individual case will be based on the information collected so that sampling methods will be impossible and a habit of mind distrustful of these methods naturally follows. This is reinforced by the fact that there is a large number of more or less independent collecting departments each of which has evolved its own habits and customs.

An important part can be played by a precise specification by economists of the information they want and the way in which they think it could be obtained from business and other records. In undertaking this often laborious task they can comfort themselves with the knowledge that nowadays, to an altogether greater extent than heretofore, their demand for *designed* information is likely to become effective because government policy and administration also have the same needs. In a world where the Chancellor of the Exchequer requires social accounting data in preparing his Budget and estimates of the future balance of payments for the long-term programme, there is a real opportunity not only for the inevitable guess-work, but also for taking seriously the whole problem of how to provide designed economic statistics. Many of these new administrative needs do not involve action arising from individual returns so that the way is open to a much greater use of modern methods of statistical collection. In this process of development a great part ought to be played, and I believe will come to be played, by the application of sampling methods to the collection of economic information.

The use of sampling methods for this purpose has been intensively studied in recent years.*

* A comprehensive account of modern sampling methods has been given in *Sampling Methods for Censuses and Surveys* (1949), by F. Yates. An attempt to suggest ways in which these methods could be used for the collection of social accounting data is to be found in 'The Use of Sampling Methods in National Income Statistics and Social Accounting', by ·R. Stone, J. E. G. Utting and J. Durbin. This paper was read to the meeting of the International Statistical Institute held at Berne in September 1949 and will appear in a forthcoming issue of the Institute's *Review*.

The mathematical basis of efficient sample design and analysis is receiving and will continue for many years to receive the attention of mathematical statisticians. Statistical design and analysis are the best developed tools in the samplers' kit-bag and, because it is easier to concentrate on sampling errors, the more intractable difficulties of systematic mis-reporting and non-response have on the whole received less attention than they deserve. I mention this because the most perfectly designed sampling procedure will not give useful results if the population to be sampled refuses or is unable to co-operate.

V. DEDUCTIVELY FORMULATED THEORIES AND THEIR VERIFICATION

I now turn to the second class of question, namely that concerned with testing hypotheses or theories. The usefulness of observation and measurement in testing economic theories arises because the theorems of economics are supposed to relate to the actual world. Any economic theorem rigorously deduced from given postulates may be regarded as an hypothesis about the actual world which experience may show to be false. Indeed, the whole economic as opposed to mathematical interest in the theorem lies in its truth or falsity and not merely in its logical relationship to the postulates. But theorems which say something about the actual world cannot be derived solely from postulates which do not, but instead are purely formal in character. Consequently, the postulates which by their very nature cannot be tested directly by economic experience require to be tested by testing the theorems. This is the normal method of science and is clearly not without its difficulties from a logical point of view. For the argument runs as follows. If postulates, then theorems: as the theorems are verified, therefore the postulates are verified. But this is only true if there is a one-one relationship between the postulates and theorems which in general there will not be. Consequently, it is much easier to show that a theory is false than that it is highly probable that it is true.

It has been suggested that economics, unlike the natural sciences, can and in fact does proceed by a direct verification of the postulates.* If this were possible it would indeed be a great gain since we could avoid the fallacy of affirming the consequent noted above. I shall return to this question after a brief treatment, by way of example, of the theory of choice.

The theory of choice, or preference, is perhaps the most highly developed branch of economics and is of particular interest since, like many branches of the natural sciences, it possesses a fully worked out, deductively formulated theory.† Such a theory, by which I mean one

---

* See L. C. Robbins, op. cit. and *The Logic of the Sciences and the Humanities* (1947), by F. S. C. Northrop, especially pp. 247 et seq.

† For a more detailed discussion of this term see Northrop, op. cit., especially chapters IV and VI.

in which the theorems are rigorously deduced from an initial set of objects and relationships which are concepts by postulation, does not in economics or any other empirical science suddenly arise in the mind of a great philosopher without any considerations of an empirical kind. Rather the procedure is somewhat as follows.*

Observation shows that in years when the supply of some important commodity like wheat is deficient the price tends to be unusually high. This leads to the generalization that other things being equal the amount demanded tends to vary inversely with the price. It is later recognized that other prices and income will affect the amount demanded. At this point, with a similar analysis on the supply side, it is possible to set out in the manner of Walras a system of relationships in terms of which the static equilibrium values of all prices and quantities could in principle be calculated. This is all on the assumption that tastes and the conditions of nature do not change.

Let us now concentrate on the demand side. It finally comes to be realized that the behaviour of consumers as already conceived can be deduced and elaborated on the basis of a small number of postulates. The essential ones are the properties of the relationships of preference and indifference and the assumption that an individual can say of any pair of combinations of goods α_r and α_s either that he prefers α_r to α_s or α_s to α_r or that he is indifferent as between the two.† These postulates may seem fairly harmless but it is obvious that they are not purely formal but express assumptions about human behaviour. They may or may not be true of the actual world and consequently any theorems based on a system of postulates of which they form a necessary part may or may not hold good in practice.

However, if we are of a mathematical turn of mind, we may now forget what it was that we originally intended to convey by the α's and by the relationships of preference and indifference. We may take certain objects and relationships with appropriate formal properties, combine them with any other postulates we may consider to be desirable and work out a purely mathematical theory in terms of the unknown objects and relationships.‡ This theory will consist of the postulates and a number of theorems logically deducible from them. But so far the results will be not economics but mathematics, though doubtless mathematics of a not very interesting kind. The essential step needed to convert the above into an economic theory is to associate the objects and relationships in the mathematical theory with corresponding economic objects and relationships. But as soon as we do this we come back to a position in which our postulates, being after all only postulates, may be false and hence lead to falsity in the theorems.

* For an account of the development in the case of the theory of consumers' choice see *The Theory and Measurement of Demand* (1938), by H. Schultz, ch. 1.

† For an elaboration of these assumptions see the following section.

‡ A simple way in which this can be done and theorems corresponding to those of the theory of choice deduced is given in the following section.

An attempt has been made by certain writers already mentioned to avoid the necessity for testing the theorems by applying a test direct to the postulates. On the face of it this seems an odd procedure, since it would seem to imply that the postulates are not really postulates at all but theorems based on some more fundamental but unstated postulates. These writers point out that it is not the collections of goods that are being ordered by the relationship of preference but the subjective valuations of these collections. Consequently, they assert, the essential postulates can be tested by introspection since we are concerned only with the individual act of ordering and not with the actual order reached in any case. But it seems to me that this will not do. I should doubt if introspection would confirm in anyone's mind that even he could in all circumstances express preference in accordance with the postulates stated above. Still less, and this is the real point, should I have thought that introspection could provide the necessary information about other individuals. Thus any attempt in this sense to test the postulates by introspection would seem to me foredoomed to failure, to be a purely private method incapable of carrying general conviction to reasonable people. The most such a method could do would be, in my view, to provide a prima facie case for supposing that the psychological basis of the theory of choice was not outrageous and that the postulates if not strictly and universally true were at any rate a plausible starting-point for further analysis.

If the view is held that the postulates, however expressed, of a theory of choice must imply something about human capacities then it seems clear that, while the attempt to test them through introspection must be abandoned, it is always possible that they can be derived as theorems in a theory not of economics but of psychology. If this could be done and if the theory in question could, by the testing of other theorems, be confirmed, then it would be possible to test the postulates of the theory of choice by the usual method employed in the sciences.

I suppose there must be a considerable literature known to psychologists which has a bearing on this point. The main papers known to me are those by Thurstone* and one by Kendall and Babington Smith† in which an attempt was made to test the transitivity of the preferences of individual children for school subjects and to investigate the consistency of the preferences displayed. The conclusion reached was that both boys and girls are genuinely capable of exercising judgements of choice which on the whole are consistent. It was found, in the very small samples investigated, that girls are less consistent and less alike in their preferences than boys.

I have tried to make clear in this brief sketch of the nature of de-

* See 'The Indifference Function', in *Journal of Social Psychology*, vol. II (1931), pp. 139–67, and 'The Prediction of Choice', in *Psychometrika*, vol. X, no. 4 (December 1945), pp. 237–54.

† See 'On the Method of Paired Comparisons', by M. G. Kendall and B. Babington Smith in *Biometrika*, vol. XXXI, pts. III and IV (March 1940), pp. 324–45.

ductively formulated theories, at least as they occur in economics, that, although their origin lies in common observation and introspection, nevertheless they are capable of a purely mathematical development through the exact statement of a set of postulates which, however, since they must inevitably contain assumptions about human behaviour, require to be tested by reference to actual events. The verification of all theories concerned with the actual world consists essentially in satisfying ourselves that for practical purposes the actual world behaves as if the postulates of the theory held true in it. If possible we should like to conduct the process of testing or verification in such a way that we could detect any individual weak links in the initial set of postulates. There is no hope, as far as I can see, of pushing the postulates of economic theory back to a set of irreducible axioms. This is not even possible in the case of geometry, although the verification that the postulates of Euclidean geometry form a satisfactory basis for ordinary everyday measurements in space has been made so often that they are never questioned from a common-sense point of view. In other spheres, e.g. cosmology, it is convenient to use geometries founded on different systems of postulates.

I shall discuss in Sections xxii–xxvii, along with certain other questions, the problem of testing one important branch of economic theory in a particular way, namely the theory of market demand for consumers' goods by observations relating to successive periods of time. The point of departure is the theory of individual preference, the relationships of which can be summed over a population of individuals to give the corresponding market relationships. A difficulty appears immediately inasmuch as the economic theory of preference is seriously incomplete. As we have already seen it is concerned with certain consistencies in the act of ordering valuations but not with the precise order achieved. This order, whatever it may be in any individual case, is assumed to remain constant. Evidently, over time, tastes and habits are likely to change and some provision, however crude, must be made for this contingency. It will be clear from the analysis I shall give that if we are interested in the theory of demand and not merely in the aspect of it which economists have concentrated on, we have still a lot to learn. Unfortunately, the other aspects of demand do not seem to have been very intensively studied by historians or sociologists.

VI. POSTULATES FOR THE THEORY OF CHOICE

Let there be a set A of elements α with non-negative components a_i, $i = 1, 2, ..., n$. Given a unit of measurement for each a an α is defined for, and only for, combinations of discrete values of the a_i.

Let there be two relationships connecting the α's. One of these, denoted by $\leftrightarrow$, is an equivalence relationship and so is *reflexive*, i.e. for each element α_r of A

$$\alpha_r \leftrightarrow \alpha_r, \tag{1}$$

symmetric, i.e. for two elements α_r and α_s of A

$$\alpha_r \leftrightarrow \alpha_s \quad \text{implies} \quad \alpha_s \leftrightarrow \alpha_r, \tag{2}$$

transitive, i.e. for three elements α_r, α_s and α_t of A

$$\alpha_r \leftrightarrow \alpha_s \quad \text{and} \quad \alpha_s \leftrightarrow \alpha_t \quad \text{imply} \quad \alpha_r \leftrightarrow \alpha_t. \tag{3}$$

The second relationship, denoted by $\rightarrow$, is

asymmetric, i.e. for two elements α_r and α_s of A

$$\alpha_r \rightarrow \alpha_s \quad \text{implies} \quad \alpha_s \nrightarrow \alpha_r, \tag{4}$$

transitive, i.e. for three elements α_r, α_s and α_t of A

$$\alpha_r \rightarrow \alpha_s \quad \text{and} \quad \alpha_s \rightarrow \alpha_t \quad \text{imply} \quad \alpha_r \rightarrow \alpha_t, \tag{5}$$

from which it follows that it is

irreflexive, i.e. for each element α_r of A

$$\alpha_r \nrightarrow \alpha_r. \tag{6}$$

Let each pair of α's be connected by one or other of these relationships so that if α_r and α_s are any two elements of A then either

$$\left. \begin{array}{l} \alpha_r \leftrightarrow \alpha_s \\ \alpha_r \rightarrow \alpha_s \\ \alpha_s \rightarrow \alpha_r \end{array} \right\}. \tag{7}$$

or
or

We may use the relationship $\leftrightarrow$ to partition A into distinct subsets (equivalence classes), A_r, $r = 1, 2, ..., N$. In virtue of this we may apply the relationship $\rightarrow$ to subsets. For if any $\alpha_r \in A_r \rightarrow$ to any $\alpha_s \in A_s$ then the relationship must hold for each α_r with respect to each α_s so that we may write $A_r \rightarrow A_s$ meaning that for any element α_r of A_r and any element α_s of A_s there holds the relationship $\alpha_r \rightarrow \alpha_s$.

Let there be a function μ linear in the components of the α's. Then μ partitions A into three subsets according as $\sum_i a_{ri} p_i \gtreqless \mu$, where the p_i are given positive constants the same for each α. The p_i, $i = 1, 2, ..., n$, are components of an object $\Pi \in$ a given set P.

Let us now consider the problem of selecting from A an object α_r such that $\alpha_s \nrightarrow \alpha_r$ subject to conditions that $\sum_i a_{ri} p_i \leqslant \mu$ and $\sum_i a_{si} p_i \leqslant \mu$, where the p_i are elements of a given Π in P. To do this, we must link the relationship $\alpha_r \rightarrow \alpha_s$ with the magnitude of the elements of the α's. The assumption we shall make to do this is that if two α's differ only in one component a_i, then

$$a_{ri} > a_{si} \text{ implies } \alpha_r \rightarrow \alpha_s. \tag{8}$$

Then for each equivalence class A_r we denote by α_{r_0} the element (or set of elements) for which, given Π, $\sum_i a_{ri} p_i$ is a minimum. We thus get a set of minimum elements α_{r_0} ($r = 1, 2, ..., N$), from which we shall select that element (or set of elements) which, for the given Π, gives the greatest $\sum\limits_{i} a_{r_i} p_i$ not exceeding μ.

Let us first restrict ourselves to the elements α_r of a given equivalence class A_r. As above, we denote by α_{r_0} the element (or set of elements) selected for a given Π, say Π_0. Let us assume that $\alpha'_{r_0} \neq 0$, i.e. that the complement of α_{r_0} in A_r is not empty, and take any element of α'_{r_0}, say α_{r_1}. Let us further assume that every element of A is selected for some value of Π and denote by Π_1 the value of Π for which α_{r_1} is a minimum element. Then

$$\sum_{i} a_{r_0 i} p_{0i} < \sum_{i} a_{r_1 i} p_{0i} \tag{9}$$

and

$$\sum_{i} a_{r_1 i} p_{1i} \leqslant \sum_{i} a_{r_0 i} p_{1i}, \tag{10}$$

so that

$$\sum_{i} (a_{r_1 i} - a_{r_0 i})(p_{1i} - p_{0i}) < 0, \tag{11}$$

or in a different notation $\sum\limits_{i} \Delta a_{ri} \Delta p_i < 0. \tag{12}$

Suppose that $p_{0i} = p_{1i}$ for all $i \neq k$ and that $p_{0k} < p_{1k}$. Then all but one term in (11) are zero and we have

$$\Delta a_{rk} \Delta p_k < 0, \tag{13}$$

that is if of the p's one alone, p_k, increases then the associated component of α_r, namely a_{rk}, must necessarily decrease.

Let us now consider the elements, α_r and α_s, of two equivalence classes such that $A_r \rightarrow A_s$. Suppose that, for the element Π_0 of P, α_r is selected and that

$$\sum_{i} a_{ri} p_{0i} \leqslant \sum_{i} a_{si} p_{0i}. \tag{14}$$

Consider now a second element Π_1 of P for which α_s is selected. It follows that

$$\sum_{i} a_{si} p_{1i} < \sum_{i} a_{ri} p_{1i}, \tag{15}$$

since otherwise α_r would have been a minimum element given Π_1. Thus we may conclude that

$$\sum_{i} (a_{si} - a_{ri})(p_1 - p_{0i}) < 0, \tag{16}$$

a result similar to that obtained in (11) for elements of a given equivalence class, A_r.

These results may now be interpreted in economic terms. A represents the set of all combinations of goods and services which are available to consumers, the relationship $\leftrightarrow$ is one of indifference, the relationship $\rightarrow$ is one of preference and may be read 'is preferred to', the function μ represents the consumer's income and Π represents a given set of prices. The crucial assumption from the economic point of view is contained in (7) and it can be seen that this assumption permits A to be partitioned into equivalence classes. Also (8) implies that a consumer's preference is ordered by the magnitude of a given commodity if the amounts of all others remain fixed.

It can be seen that the results obtained are identical to those given by

Samuelson* so that 'almost all the meaningful empirical implications of the whole pure theory of consumer's choice' can be derived from the assumptions made. No assumption of continuity in the budget space is needed nor is it necessary to consider infinitely small changes of prices. Thus we need not consider such absurdities as fractional parts of motor-cars or wireless sets nor need we consider the effect of a price ratio changing from 1 to 1·0 ... 01. Instead we may restrict ourselves to such discrete values of quantities and prices as are available to the consumer in practice. An assumption corresponding to that of convexity of the indifference surfaces is introduced where it is needed, by assuming that every element of A is selected for some value of Π. This assumption is needed to obtain the usual results when we consider elements of a given A_r but is not needed when we consider the elements of two distinct equivalence classes.

VII. THE ESTIMATION OF PARAMETERS

In economics, as in other subjects, we meet with a number of different kinds of mathematical relationship. Perhaps the simplest is the definitional relationship which contains only variables linked together by the ordinary signs of arithmetic. Examples of such relationships are: income equals consumption plus saving; the sum of saving by each sector of the economy equals the total saving of the economy; the quantity of some commodity sold multiplied by the average selling price equals the expenditure on the commodity. These equations do not tell us anything about the behaviour of economic agents; they simply indicate the defined relationships between certain terms. When relationships of this kind form part of a system of equations they may be used to eliminate certain variables from the system and thus reduce the degrees of freedom of the system. To go back to the example of the definitional relationship—income equals consumption plus saving—we can obviously write down (income minus consumption) wherever saving appears in a system of relationships, thus reducing the number of variables and of equations.

Evidently, we cannot build up a theory of human behaviour with the aid of definitional relationships alone; in addition we shall need relationships of a behaviouristic or institutional character telling us something of the way in which the different individuals or institutions behave or indicating the technical relationships which subsist between, say, the input of factors of production and the output of product. Examples of such relationships are: the familiar demand and supply relationships; the relationship connecting saving to income and the rate of interest; a relationship indicating the presence or absence of price control,† that

---

* See *Foundations of Economic Analysis* (1947), pp. 107–11.

† A relationship of this type which, so far as I am aware, has not been used in the past was introduced by Marschak in a paper to the International Statistical Conferences, Washington, 1947. See 'Statistical Inference from Non-experimental Observations', summarized in *Econometrica*, vol. XVI, no. 1 (January 1948), pp. 53–5.

is the influence of an aspect of the legal system highly relevant to economic behaviour.

The feature of this whole class of relationships is that they involve in addition to the variables which enter into them certain constants or parameters. These parameters will reflect behaviour or technical and legal influences in the actual world. In the overwhelming majority of cases they will have to be estimated from observations.

This sort of parameter will in most cases tell us the extent of the influence of one variable on another. In demand analysis, for example, we shall not merely be interested to know that in the case of some commodity a rise in income will be associated, other things being equal, with a rise in consumption, but we shall want to know how big this rise will be. Thus the estimation of a parameter is involved every time we want to know the magnitude of the response to be expected from a given change. A similar estimation will in fact frequently be needed if we only wish to make purely qualitative statements. This will happen whenever the sign of a term or group of terms in a relationship is left in doubt by theory. Examples are: whether a rise in the price of a commodity will, given money income and the other prices and tastes, raise or lower the amount demanded; whether a rise in the exchange rate will raise or lower an adverse balance of payments. Theory can suggest the various influences on which the outcome depends but, unless assumptions are made about these influences or the magnitude of their effect is actually estimated, nothing can be said about even the direction of change.

In setting the matter out in this way I have, I believe, followed the usual train of thought of the economist who is not, in most aspects of his work, interested in purely empirical relationships. An exception to this statement is to be found in the development of certain empirical forecasting devices, but these can prove treacherous and are always adopted *faute de mieux*. Generally speaking the economist considers relationships in terms of some deductively formulated theory which can be put in a form in which each relationship is capable of being identified and interpreted. When he thinks of the connexion between the quantity transacted and the price of some commodity he unhesitatingly considers two relationships: one of demand, the other of supply. For most of his purposes an impossible position would result if the two got mixed up. In considering the responses of buyers it is important to know the magnitude of the influence of price in the demand relationship; it would be useless to know only some arbitrary combination of the strength of demand and supply responses, since such averages would not have any meaning. It is nevertheless only too easy to produce 'theories' which contain arbitrary parameters, the magnitude of which cannot in principle be determined from observations. Evidently we must know if this state of affairs is being encountered, since it is meaningless to attempt to estimate parameters which are arbitrary in this sense.

This is the principal problem, other than those of a purely statistical nature, which arises in the estimation of parameters and it has been much discussed in recent years under the name of the problem of identification,* although in a general way it has been known for many years.† It arises independently of any statistical considerations, that is to say it would still be present if the sizes of samples could be increased indefinitely, and it is for this reason that I have introduced it here rather than at a later stage in the discussion of statistical applications.

This problem can be seen in its simplest terms if we consider how we should estimate the parameters in, for example, the supply and demand equations for some consumers' commodity—assuming for simplicity perfect competition, constant tastes and constant natural conditions, and unlimited data in the form of observations over consecutive periods of time. The first question we may try to answer is: other things being equal, how large a change in the amount demanded would be associated with a given change in the price? Let us suppose that our theory of supply and demand states simply that the quantity demanded depends on price and an unspecified set of influences which shift the demand schedule about, that supply also depends on price and an unspecified set of influences which shift the supply schedule about, that the price equilibrates the amounts demanded and supplied, that the relationships are linear and that the shifts are free from autocorrelation. Then we may express the theory mathematically as follows:

(i) $$d_t = \alpha p_t + \epsilon_t,$$
(ii) $$s_t = \beta p_t + \eta_t,$$
(iii) $$d_t = s_t,$$

where in period t, d_t is the amount demanded, s_t is the amount supplied, p_t is the price, ϵ_t and η_t are random variables which express the shifts in the demand and supply schedules respectively and α and β are two parameters which indicate the influence of price changes on d_t and s_t respectively. If this is the theory then we must give up any attempt to estimate the magnitudes of α and β except in special circumstances. For example we could only estimate α, our original desideratum, if over time the supply curve had been shifting about while demand influences, other than price, had remained unchanged; so that, as it were, the shifting supply curve traced out a demand curve in the price-quantity plane. This is equivalent to assuming that ϵ_t is a constant and is clearly a rather unlikely state of affairs, since in fact it is to be expected that both curves will have been shifting about under the influence of factors other than price, such as income, costs, weather conditions and the like. If there are no other factors, that is if both ϵ_t and η_t are constants, then the intersecting supply and demand schedules will determine an unique price and an unique quantity so that again, since in this case

* See, for example, 'Identification Problems in Economic Model Construction', by T. C. Koopmans, in *Econometrica*, vol. XVII, no. 2 (April 1949), pp. 125–44.

† See, for example, 'Pitfalls in the Statistical Construction of Demand and Supply Curves' by R. Frisch in *Veröffentlichungen der Frankfurter Gesellschaft für Konjunkturforschung*, neue folge, heft 5, 1933, pp. 6–39.

there is no variation, it will be impossible to estimate the effect of price on either the amount demanded or the amount supplied, i.e. either α or β. Assuming that the unspecified shifts both undergo an unknown amount of variation then no amount of information of the type postulated will enable us to estimate the response of either buyers or sellers to price changes. Each relationship is said to be unidentifiable for we may make a linear combination of them in any way we like and these combinations will be indistinguishable in form from each of the original equations. The position would be different if in one relationship the amount demanded (or supplied) depended on the price in a previous period or if it were possible to specify in the supply and demand model some relationship between the shifts, e.g. that they be uncorrelated. In the former case the difference made is obvious whereas in the latter case it can readily be seen that if any linear combinations were substituted for the original equations the shifts could no longer be independent.

The position would be altered if in one equation, say the supply one, the amount supplied depended on a third factor, say rainfall. In such a case the demand equation would be identifiable while the supply equation would not. For, in the terminology used in the first example, the demand equation multiplied by any arbitrary constant could be added to the supply equation to produce an equation identical in form but with different coefficients.

A more likely situation in practice is one in which there is at least a second (and different) determining variable in each equation. In this case, provided that the parameters of the two additional determining variables are not each equal to zero, we can no longer obtain equations of identical form by taking linear combinations of the two original equations and the latter may therefore be identifiable.

The moral of this discussion is that where we think that two variables relating to a given time period are connected by more than one relationship we must be careful to introduce at least the more important determining variables which we suppose to enter into any one of the relationships under investigation. Furthermore, we must be reasonably satisfied, if we do not propose to deal with more than one relationship in a system, that the system could be completed, consistently with theory and observation, in such a way that the equation under investigation was identifiable. This will always be possible if it is thought appropriate to use sequence models, or recursive systems in the language of Bentzel and Wold.* If it is not thought that this is justified then difficulties of identification provide a powerful argument, supplemented by statistical considerations, for operating with complete systems, or models, in which the number of independent equations is equal to the number of endogenous or interacting variables. The objections to this procedure are almost wholly of a practical nature arising largely from

* See 'On Statistical Demand Analysis from the Viewpoint of Simultaneous Equations', by R. Bentzel and H. Wold, in *Skandinavisk Aktuarietidskrift* (1946), pp. 95–114.

lack of data and the very incomplete way in which certain aspects of the model, notably the form of the relationships and the time lags, are specified by theory.

In this account of the identification problem I have stressed the idea of a parameter as representing the strength of a response of some individual entity or collection of entities in the economy, although, of course, not all parameters can be interpreted in this way. This leads to the idea of a structural equation as one which reflects the behaviour or situation of a single entity or collection of entities which for the purpose in hand can be regarded as homogeneous. For example the demand and supply equations for some commodity reflect an aspect of the behaviour of the buyers and sellers of that commodity. But in this example we could eliminate price or quantity from the demand and supply relationships and obtain first a sales equation and second a price formation equation. These relationships would not reflect the behaviour of any single collection of entities but the outcome of the behaviour of two collections.

Is there any advantage in operating with structural equations? The answer is 'yes' for the following reasons. In the case of relationships expressing behaviour these may be expected to have the highest possible degree of permanence since they reflect the behaviour of only one type of entity in the system. Derived relationships, on the other hand, such as the sales and price formation equations just mentioned, depend for their stability on the constant responses not of one but of two or more types of entity; in the example, both buyers and sellers. Thus, if we can assume that the buyers' responses, though not the sellers' responses, will remain constant over a period, we can express (or forecast) the quantity transacted by using one equation if we adopt the demand equation, whereas we shall need at least two if we adopt the sales equation.

These two ideas, identification and structural relationships, indicate the importance of theory in enabling us to interpret and use the statistically determined constants in economic relationships. The dangers of neglecting theory are very real because economic variation over time tends to be gradual and because economic variables belong to a system in which they are more or less closely connected. As a result empirical relationships can readily be found to which no meaning can be assigned and crude formulations of relationships which, though sound as far as they go, are incomplete, may easily prove a very treacherous basis for empirical work.*

* This is the practical danger illustrated by the picturesque examples given by statisticians in discussing the problem of nonsense correlations. No real danger arises in these examples. For instance Yule found from annual data a correlation of 0·95 over the period 1866–1911 between the standardized mortality rate in England and Wales and the proportion of Church of England marriages. The nonsense here is so evident that the demographer is hardly likely to be led astray. See 'Why do we Sometimes get Nonsense Correlations Between Time Series', by G. U. Yule, in *Journal of the Royal Statistical Society*, vol. LXXXIX, pt. 1 (1926), pp. 1–64.

VIII. THE NATURE OF PREDICTION

Prediction in one of its many forms is the goal of economics as it is of other sciences concerned with the actual world. But prediction may be attempted in so many different ways which are logically distinct that it will probably be best if I begin by discussing and illustrating the basis needed for a full prediction even if this ideal is still a long way from being realized in practical work.

Prediction in this sense requires that we can define the state of the system, or some part of it, in terms of a knowledge of the values of certain variables and that we possess a dynamic theory by means of which we can derive future states of the system by logical implication from a knowledge of the present state. In terms of a saving-investment example which I shall use as an illustration, this means that we have, let us say, a system of relationships connecting saving, investment and income of such a kind that if we know the parameters of the system and the present values of the three variables we can deduce the values which these variables will take in each future period.

If we are to be able to do this it is evident that the values of the variables connected by the relationships of the system must not all relate simply to the levels of those variables in a single period of time. A system of this kind would be static and its solution would yield only the equilibrium values of the variables. In physics it is usual to make this connexion between consecutive periods by reducing to the limit the length of the period and by introducing derivatives of the first and higher orders, i.e. rates of change, accelerations and so forth. In economics on the other hand the differential equations of physics are commonly replaced by finite-difference equations, i.e. dx/dt is replaced by $\Delta x/\Delta t$, where Δt is some unit period, say the month or the year. In this way past values of at least some of the variables are introduced into the system and a link is thus created between the past and the present and, by extension, between the present and the future.

IX. A SIMPLE MODEL

To illustrate these ideas let me write out a simple, indeed an intentionally over-simplified, saving-investment model,* involving only three variables and three relationships. I shall assume that the variables and the parameters in the model can be estimated without error and in the first place that the relationships themselves hold exactly. On this understanding let X_1 be consumption outlay and X_3 be income and let small letters, x_i, stand for deviations from means. Furthermore, let E be an operator† which when applied to a variable displaces it by one time

* See a note of mine entitled 'Lord Keynes: the New Theory of Money', in *Nature*, vol. CLVIII (9 November 1946), p. 652.
† See, for example, *Calculus of Finite Differences* (2nd edit. 1947), by C. Jordan, ch. I.

unit so that $E^n x_t \equiv x_{t+n}$ and $E^{-n} x_t \equiv x_{t-n}$. Obviously in this notation $E^0 x_t \equiv x_t$ so that in this case it will be convenient to omit the operator. Then, in its exact form, a very simple propensity-to-consume relationship might be written as

$$x_1 = aE^{-1} x_3, \tag{17}$$

if we let X_4 stand for saving and adopt the definition $x_4 \equiv x_3 - x_1$; then the corresponding saving-income relationship is

$$x_4 = (1 - aE^{-1}) x_3. \tag{18}$$

Finally, we introduce X_2 as asset formation (or investment) and suppose that the variations in it depend linearly on last year's income and the rate at which last year's income was changing. Then the investment-income relationship may be written

$$x_2 = (bE^{-1} + cE^{-2}) x_3. \tag{19}$$

These two relationships express the relevant aspect of the behaviour of two groups in the community, the savers and the investors. The system is closed by the definitional relationship or accounting identity of the form

$$x_4 \equiv x_2. \tag{20}$$

Before going on to an analysis of this example let us first look at the model consisting of (18), (19) and (20) from the standpoint of identification. Equation (20) is an identity, so we do not need to worry about identification in its case and we may concentrate attention on (18) and (19). The condition for the exact identifiability of a structural equation in a linear model is that the number of variables which appear in the model but do not appear in the equation be equal to the number of equations in the model less one. In the present case we have five variables, x_2, x_3, $E^{-1} x_3$, $E^{-2} x_3$ and x_4 and three equations. Accordingly to be identifiable (18) and (19) must each contain three variables as in fact they do, (18) containing x_3, $E^{-1} x_3$ and x_4 and (19) containing x_2, $E^{-1} x_3$ and $E^{-2} x_3$. Thus the parameters a, b and c are identifiable.

How are we to use this model for purposes of prediction? One way we might proceed is as follows. If we know the values of x_2, x_3 and x_4 at time t then from (18) we can derive the value of $E^{-1} x_3$. Equating the right-hand sides of (18) and (19) we obtain

$$[1 - (a + b) E^{-1} - cE^{-2}] x_3 = 0, \tag{21}$$

and substituting x_3 and $E^{-1} x_3$ for $E^{-1} x_3$ and $E^{-2} x_3$ in this equation we obtain the value of Ex_3, that is the value of x_3 at time $(t+1)$. Evidently we may proceed indefinitely in this way and then, knowing the values of x_3 at different times in the future, we can easily obtain the values of x_2 and x_4 from (18) and (19). Reflexion will show that equation (21) would also hold if x_2 or x_4 were substituted for x_3 so that in fact (21) is the fundamental autoregressive equation of the system.* In fact the term in square brackets in (21) is simply the determinant of the matrix of the coefficients (polynomials in the operator E) of the x_i obtained by writing (18), (19) and (20) in homogeneous form. Thus writing $[\alpha(E)]$ for the matrix of coefficients in a system of linear difference equations in homogeneous form the autoregressive structure of the system is given by the expression $|\alpha(E)|\, x_i = 0$.

X. THE DEVELOPMENT OF A LINEAR MODEL OVER TIME

The question of how a system like the above will develop over time has been treated by Tinbergen.† An equation of the form

$$(1 - \alpha_1 E^{-1} - \ldots - \alpha_n E^{-n})\, x_i = 0 \qquad (22)$$

is called a difference equation of the nth order. Since my simple model gives rise to a difference equation of the second order we may conveniently take this as an example. From the equation

$$(1 - \alpha_1 E^{-1} - \alpha_2 E^{-2})\, x_i = 0, \qquad (23)$$

we can form the *characteristic equation*

$$y^2 - \alpha_1 y - \alpha_2 = 0, \qquad (24)$$

with roots λ_1 and λ_2 of the form

$$\lambda_1 = \frac{\alpha_1}{2} + \left(\frac{\alpha_1^2}{4} + \alpha_2\right)^{\frac{1}{2}} \qquad (25)$$

and

$$\lambda_2 = \frac{\alpha_1}{2} - \left(\frac{\alpha_1^2}{4} + \alpha_2\right)^{\frac{1}{2}}. \qquad (26)$$

When expressed as functions of time, the variables in (23) will be of the form

$$E^n x_i = A_1 \lambda_1^n + A_2 \lambda_2^n. \qquad (27)$$

Since the coefficients α_1 and α_2 are real numbers, the roots λ_1 and λ_2 are either both real or they are conjugate complex, the latter case arising

---

* See 'Prediction from Autoregressive Schemes and Linear Stochastic Difference Systems', by J. R. N. Stone, to appear in vol. III of the *Proceedings of the International Statistical Conferences, Washington*, 1947, and also 'A Study of the Autoregressive Nature of the Time Series used for Tinbergen's Model of the Economic System of the United States, 1919–1932', by G. H. Orcutt, in *Journal of the Royal Statistical Society* (Series B), vol. X, no. 1 (1948), pp. 1–45.

† See *Statistical Testing of Business Cycle Theories, II. Business Cycles in the United States of America*, 1919–1932 (1939), by J. Tinbergen, especially ch. VI, and 'Ligevaegtstyper og konjunkturbevaegelse', by J. Tinbergen, in *Nordisk Tidsskrift for Teknisk Økonomi* (January 1944). See also 'Expressing the Stability of an Economy by Means of Difference Equations' (in Dutch), by H. Rijken van Olst, in *Statistische en Econometrische Onderzoekingen*, jaargang 3, no. 3 (March 1948), pp. 12–24.

when the term in round brackets in (25), termed the discriminant, is negative. If we are given two values of x_i, say x_i and Ex_i, we can calculate A_1 and A_2.

If the roots are real we have simply

$$A_1 + A_2 = x_i, \tag{28}$$

$$A_1 \lambda_1 + A_2 \lambda_2 = Ex_i, \tag{29}$$

from which we obtain
$$A_1 = \frac{(E - \lambda_2)}{(\lambda_1 - \lambda_2)} x_i \tag{30}$$

and
$$A_2 = \frac{(\lambda_1 - E)}{(\lambda_1 - \lambda_2)} x_i, \tag{31}$$

whence
$$E^n x_i = \frac{(E - \lambda_2)}{(\lambda_1 - \lambda_2)} x_i \lambda_1^n + \frac{(\lambda_1 - E)}{(\lambda_1 - \lambda_2)} x_i \lambda_2^n. \tag{32}$$

If the roots λ_1 and λ_2 are complex they will be of the form $(\lambda + i\lambda')$ and $(\lambda - i\lambda')$ or $ke^{i\theta}$ and $ke^{-i\theta}$, where $k = (\lambda^2 + \lambda'^2)^{\frac{1}{2}}$ and $\theta = \tan^{-1} \lambda'/\lambda$. In this case we may put

$$A_1 = L_1 + iL_1' \tag{33}$$

and
$$A_2 = L_2 + iL_2'. \tag{34}$$

Then for x_i real, $i(L_1' + L_2') = 0$ or $L_1' = -L_2' = L'$, say. Also for Ex_i real, $i(L_1 \sin \theta + L_2 \sin -\theta) = 0$ or $L_1 = L_2 = L$, say. Then

$$E^n x_i = (L + iL')(ke^{i\theta})^n + (L - iL')(ke^{-i\theta})^n$$
$$= k^n[(L + iL')(\cos n\theta + i \sin n\theta) + (L - iL')(\cos n\theta - i \sin n\theta)]$$
$$= k^n(\Lambda \cos n\theta - \Lambda' \sin n\theta), \tag{35}$$

where $\Lambda = 2L$ and $\Lambda' = 2L'$ can be determined. For, writing

$$k(\Lambda \cos \theta - \Lambda' \sin \theta) \quad \text{in the form} \quad \Lambda \lambda - \Lambda' \lambda',$$

we have
$$\Lambda \cos 0 = x_i, \tag{36}$$

$$\Lambda \lambda - \Lambda' \lambda' = Ex_i, \tag{37}$$

from which we obtain
$$\Lambda = x_i \tag{38}$$

and
$$\Lambda' = \frac{(\lambda - E)}{\lambda'} x_i, \tag{39}$$

whence
$$E^n x_i = \frac{(\lambda^2 + \lambda'^2)^{n/2}}{\lambda'} [\lambda' x_i \cos n\theta - (\lambda - E) x_i \sin n\theta]. \tag{40}$$

If disturbed from equilibrium (with $x_i = 0$ for all i) a linear system may tend back to the equilibrium values of the variables or tend away from these equilibrium values, or it may oscillate with constant, increasing or decreasing amplitude. A system which tends to return quickly to the equilibrium values of its variables is said to be highly damped while a system which tends rapidly away from them is said to be highly anti-damped.

XI. PREDICTION AND ECONOMIC POLICY

Returning to the highly simplified example of equations (18), (19) and (20) let me attempt to show how the information it contains might be used for policy purposes. A system with the autoregressive structure shown in (21) will oscillate if the discriminant

$$\tfrac{1}{4}(a+b)^2+c<0. \tag{41}$$

Let us suppose that in the example $a=0.6$, $b=1.0$ and $c=-1.0$. These values correspond to a system showing undamped oscillations with a period of about ten time units. Suppose that the government observe these oscillations and wish to remove them. One way in which this could be done would be to introduce a tax and transfer payment scheme so that the disposable income of consumers would no longer be x_3 but, say (x_3-x_5), where x_5 is the amount of the tax and would be negative if the government wished to raise income above the earnings of consumers. Thus we will suppose that (x_3-x_5) replaces x_3 in (18) while (19) and (20) remain the same. We now have four variables but only three equations so we will add a fourth,

$$(1-E^{-1})x_3=0, \tag{42}$$

expressing the government's policy objective of keeping consumers' earnings ≡ national product constant from year to year. The evaluation of the determinant $|\alpha(E)|$ for this new system yields the autoregressive structure

$$[1-(1+a)E^{-1}+aE^{-2}]x_i=0. \tag{43}$$

In this case the discriminant $\tfrac{1}{4}(1-a)^2$ cannot be negative and so the system will no longer oscillate.* Since the original system was identifiable the values of a, b and c could in principle be estimated without ambiguity and so, since the above result depends on the value of a, we can see in this case the importance of an identifiable system. All that remains to be done is to calculate the successive values of x_5 needed to stabilize the system, and this is possible from a knowledge of the state of the system when the stabilizing scheme is introduced together with the equations describing the structure of the system after the introduction of the stabilizing policy.

To illustrate the whole process before and after government intervention let us assume that a system as given by (18), (19) and (20) with $a=0.6$, $b=1.0$ and $c=-1.0$, which has been running at its mean value (with $x_i=0$ for all i), is disturbed. We will assume that, in year 0, x_3 is pushed by some influence not in the system to the value 5. From

---

* In this example it is fairly safe to suppose that $0<a<1$ quite apart from the particular value here assumed for a.

equations (18) to (20) we can calculate the values of each of the variables over each future time period and as already described they will start to oscillate as a consequence of the single disturbance. Taking x_1 as an example, we have $\lambda = 0.8$, $\lambda' = 0.6$, $E^3 x_1 = 4.68$ and $E^4 x_1 = 2.70$: whence, written in the form of (35), we have for future values of x_1

$$E^n x_1 = 4.68 \cos (n-3)\, \theta - 1.74 \sin (n-3)\, \theta, \tag{44}$$

where $\theta = \tan^{-1} \frac{3}{4}$.

In the eleventh year after the disturbance income, x_3, will return approximately to a peak value after a great depression. The government may wish to stabilize income at this level and may attempt to do so by the fiscal policy device already discussed, in which case the model after intervention would take the form

$$x_1 = 0.6E^{-1}(x_3 - x_5), \tag{45}$$

$$x_2 = (E^{-1} - E^{-2})\, x_3, \tag{46}$$

$$(1 - E^{-1})\, x_3 = 0, \tag{47}$$

$$x_4 = (1 - 0.6E^{-1})\, (x_3 - x_5), \tag{48}$$

$$x_4 = x_2, \tag{49}$$

yielding the autoregressive structure

$$(1 - 1.6E^{-1} + 0.6E^{-2})\, x_i = 0. \tag{50}$$

The course of the variables before and after intervention is shown in Table 1 and the accompanying diagram.

It will be observed that before and after intervention the behaviour patterns of the community are the same; the only difference is that after intervention consumers have to reckon with the new tax, that is their disposable income is less than their earnings, while the government adjusts the level of the tax with the object of stabilizing total income in the sense of earnings.

What will happen as a result of the intervention can be seen from the diagram. Income is stabilized at the level it reached just before intervention which in this case is 8·27 units above its old average level. Saving and asset formation soon fall back to their normal level since in the second year after intervention $(E^{-1} - E^{-2})\, x_3 = 0$ and remain at this level thereafter. Consumption, after an initial rise, gradually falls back asymptotically to its average level. The tax rises slowly in the first year and more sharply in the second and finally approaches asymptotically to a level which is equal to the excess of the new level of income above its average level before the government intervention. In other words, with this method of introducing stability, the government will eventually have to levy a tax equal to the difference between the old average level of income and the higher stabilized level.

But, you may ask, what will the government do with the proceeds of the tax? The answer is that as the model is set out it will have to spend

TABLE 1. DEVELOPMENT OF HYPOTHETICAL MODEL WHEN DISTURBED BEFORE AND AFTER GOVERNMENT INTERVENTION

n	x_1	x_2	x_3	x_4	x_5
−1	0	0	0	0	0
0	...	...	5·00	...	0
1	3·00	5·00	8·00	5·00	0
2	4·80	3·00	7·80	3·00	0
3	4·68	−0·18	4·50	−0·18	0
4	2·70	−3·30	−0·60	−3·30	0
5	−0·36	−5·14	−5·50	−5·14	0
6	−3·30	−4·90	−8·20	−4·90	0
7	−4·92	−2·68	−7·60	−2·68	0
8	−4·56	0·56	−4·00	0·56	0
9	−2·40	3·60	1·20	3·60	0
10	0·72	5·18	5·90	5·18	0
11	3·54	4·73	8·27	4·73	0
12	4·96	2·37	8·27	2·37	0·94
13	4·40	0	8·27	0	3·87
14	2·64	0	8·27	0	5·63
15	1·58	0	8·27	0	6·68
16	0·95	0	8·27	0	7·32
17	0·57	0	8·27	0	7·70
18	0·34	0	8·27	0	7·93
19	0·21	0	8·27	0	8·07
20	0·12	0	8·27	0	8·15
∞	0	0	8·27	0	8·27

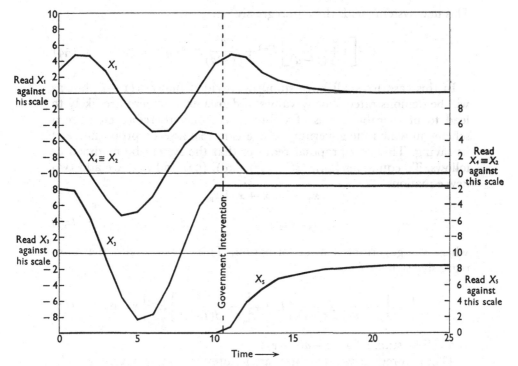

DIAGRAM 1. Development of Hypothetical Model when disturbed before and after Government Intervention

the entire proceeds on goods and services. This is fairly obvious since it can be seen from Table I that consumption + asset formation + tax = income. However, it may be instructive to consider various alternatives.

Suppose that without working the matter out someone in the government has the intuitive idea that since a tax is going to be imposed to stabilize the system, the government ought to do some saving since otherwise there will not be enough private saving out of income after the tax has been deducted to finance private asset formation. To demonstrate the result of this idea we must introduce two new variables, x_6 = government current expenditure on goods and services, and x_7 = government saving. There is no government asset formation, for the whole point of the government saving is to make good the intuitively expected lack of private saving. We will assume that the policy is to be that the government will save a proportion d of the proceeds of the tax.

This new proposal is represented by a system composed of equations (45) to (48) plus the following three new equations

$$x_3 = x_1 + x_2 + x_6, \tag{51}$$

$$x_5 = x_6 + x_7, \tag{52}$$

$$x_7 = dx_5. \tag{53}$$

This new system yields the autoregressive structure

$$\left\{ I - \left[I + \frac{a}{(I-d)} \right] E^{-1} + \frac{a}{(I-d)} E^{-2} \right\} x_i = 0. \tag{54}$$

In this case we shall have stability provided that $a \leqslant (I-d)$, but as will be demonstrated shortly values of d greater than zero are likely to lead to undesirable forms of stability. We may therefore envisage a scheme in which the government invests in real assets a proportion e of its saving. This new proposal requires that the system be modified as follows. To equations (45), (46), (47), (48), (52) and (53) we add two new equations

$$x_3 = x_1 + x_2 + x_6 + x_8, \tag{55}$$

$$x_8 = ex_7, \tag{56}$$

where x_8 = government asset formation. This system yields the autoregressive structure

$$\left\{ I - \left[I + \frac{a}{I - d(I-e)} \right] E^{-1} + \left[\frac{a}{I - d(I-e)} \right] E^{-2} \right\} x_i = 0, \tag{57}$$

and will be stable if $a \leqslant I - d(I-e)$.

The autoregressive structure after intervention is given, on the different hypotheses, by (50), (54) and (57). In all cases the roots are of the form $\lambda_1 = 1$, and $\lambda_2 = \omega$, say, where ω is real. Thus from (32) we have in each case

$$E^n x_i = \frac{(E - \omega)}{(1 - \omega)} x_i + \frac{(1 - E)}{(1 - \omega)} x_i \omega^n. \qquad (58)$$

For stability it is necessary that $\omega \leqslant 1$ for if $\omega > 1$ then $E^n x_i$ increases without limit. If $\omega = 1$ then $E^n x_i = x_i$, i.e. x_i will remain constant at its initial value. If $\omega < 1$ then $E^n x_i$ will tend asymptotically to the value

$$(Ex_i - \omega x_i)/(1 - \omega).$$

In the first case of intervention considered without government saving and investment we have $\omega = a = 0.6$. Then each x_i will tend in time to the value

$$2.5(Ex_i - 0.6x_i).$$

Thus, for example, we obtain from the data for periods 13 and 14 of Table 1:

$$\text{limit of } x_1 = 0,$$
$$\text{limit of } x_5 = 8.27.$$

In the second case of intervention with government saving we have $\omega = a/(1 - d)$ and it is assumed that $0 \leqslant d < 1$. Thus for stability we must have $0 < a \leqslant (1 - d) < 1$ or with $a = 0.6$ we require $0 < d \leqslant 0.4$. If we put $d = 0.4$ we shall ensure that x_i remains constant at its initial value. For other values of d consistent with stability, x_i tends in time to the value

$$\frac{(1 - d) Ex_i - ax_i}{1 - (a + d)}.$$

Thus, given that $a = 0.6$, d can be adjusted, within its prescribed range, to give various limiting values of the x_i. For example, if $a = 0.6$ and $d = 0.25$, we have $\omega = 0.8$ so that each x_i will tend in time to the value

$$5.0(Ex_i - 0.8x_i).$$

Thus we may calculate that

$$\text{limit of } x_1 = -8.27,$$
$$\text{limit of } x_3 = 8.27,$$
$$\text{limit of } x_4 = -5.52,$$
$$\text{limit of } x_5 = 22.08,$$

a result which could hardly be intended. If we had $d > 0.4$ the position would be much worse. To maintain the stability of income the government would be forced to impose a tax that grew larger and larger through time while private consumption and saving became larger and larger negative deviations from their old average. Of course if such a policy were pursued the economic, not to say the political, structure would break down, but the analysis shows the implications of a policy which might have some appeal to the layman if these implications were not made clear.

In the third case of intervention with government asset formation as well as saving we have $\omega = a/[1 - d(1 - e)]$. Since we may assume that

$0 \leqslant d < 1$ and $0 \leqslant e < 1$ we must have for stability $0 < a \leqslant [1 - d(1-e)] < 1$. Thus with $a = 0.6$ we require $e \geqslant [1 - (0.4/d)]$ so that, for example, if the government is to save 50 per cent of its revenue it must invest in real assets at least 20 per cent of its saving.

XII. PRACTICAL OBJECTIONS TO EXACT MODELS

Now apart from the difficulties of formulating a realistic model, of measuring the variables it contains and of estimating the parameters that enter into it, there can be no doubt that in economics weighty objections can be raised against any simple approach of this kind. For, in the first place, it is quite unthinkable in practice that the relationships other than the definitions should be satisfied exactly. However much trouble we go to in making a long list of determining variables for each behaviouristic equation it is not to be expected that such lists will be complete. Rather we shall try to introduce in each case the main systematic influences and leave aside a vast number of minor variables the effects of which will tend as a rule to cancel out. In the second place the adoption of a model like the above involves the tacit assumption that the system which it represents has functioned and will continue to function in the same way. It may be however that we know that it will not. Both these questions must be considered in more detail.

We may think of the influence of omitted variables as shocks or disturbances which prevent the smooth development of the movement shown by the exact equations. This may be explicitly recognized by adding an ϵ, representing a random disturbance, to the right-hand side of each of the behaviouristic equations with the result that some linear combination of these disturbances will appear in place of the zero on the right-hand side of (21). When this is done it is possible to represent certain new types of variation. The movement of a system governed by a set of linear stochastic difference equations may be of a quasi-oscillatory character despite the fact that the systematic component is not oscillatory. It is also possible for the system to wander without possessing any mean or equilibrium value. In fact Orcutt has suggested* on the basis of an analysis of Tinbergen's data that the American economy may be of this wandering type expressed by the autoregressive equation

$$(1 - 1.3E^{-1} + 0.3E^{-2})\, x_i = \epsilon_i. \tag{59}$$

Segments of a series generated by this equation look very much like segments of a typical economic time series.† The introduction of the ϵ's, however, has an important bearing on prediction. In making a mechanical forecast from a stochastic model the only thing to do is to assume

* Op. cit. pp. 29 et seq.
† See 'Testing the Significance of Correlation between Time Series', by G. H. Orcutt and S. F. James, in *Biometrika*, vol. xxxv, pts. III and IV (December 1948), pp. 397–413.

all future values of the disturbances equal to their expected value, zero, and to consider the future development from the given position as indicated by the systematic component of the system. Since we have every reason to believe that the future disturbances will in fact take on not zero values but values distributed around zero as in the past, predictions based on a scheme of the general type of (59) will tend to become subject to a growing margin of error as the time interval back to the present increases.* In fact in the long run the error variance of a prediction will tend to the variance of the variable predicted. With a wandering scheme like (59) (with the autoregressive parameters shown) this variance will increase without limit. As I suggested in Section 1 above this is the point at which the econometrician should call in the practical economist who may be able to hazard some opinion about the probable influence of specific disturbances that are likely to be operative between the present time and the date to which the prediction relates. Without such aid it is quite possible to make predictions, but their reliability will tend to decrease progressively as they are pursued further and further into the future.

Let us come now to the second practical difficulty which I mentioned above, namely what we are to do if the system represented by the model ceases to function in the same way. This problem is of special importance in a partly planned economy in which the government is constantly under the necessity of preventing certain variables from being determined by the old set of factors and can conveniently be discussed in terms of the idea of degrees of freedom.

If we have n variables supposed to be exactly related by n equations we may assign to them n degrees of freedom in each time period since without some restriction on the joint distribution of the variables the value of each of them in a given period may be assigned at will. The equations, however, will restrict the joint values and if they are exact will in total absorb all the degrees of freedom so that no values can be assigned at will. In an economic system containing n variables the degrees of freedom will be reduced to $(n-m)$ if there are m independent relationships of a definitional kind; for example, accounting identities. The remaining degrees of freedom will be absorbed by technical, behaviouristic and institutional relationships.

In a free market economy these degrees of freedom will in the main be absorbed by the behaviouristic relationships of the community, those absorbed by government action being reduced to a minimum. The degrees of freedom controlled by the community will be absorbed by relationships which may be supposed with a reasonable degree of realism to remain fairly stable, their form and parameters changing, as a rule, only slowly over time. Changes will certainly occur with new techniques, new products and new markets; but if we concentrate on aggregates the effect of the change over short periods is likely to be

* See the summary of my paper to the International Statistical Conferences, in *Econometrica*, vol. XVI, no. 1 (January 1948), pp. 38–40.

small. Then if we can determine the laws of motion of such a system we may reasonably hope to make at any rate short-term predictions.

If on the other hand all the degrees of freedom are controlled by the government we again reach a position in which it should be possible to make satisfactory short-run predictions. The sort of equation to be met with in such a system would, however, be different from those described above. The behaviouristic relationships of the community would be replaced by an equal number of equations each showing a variable equal to some constant, its planned value. In this case we should have to discover not the laws of motion of the system but the objectives of the government. Of course this objective might be to reproduce the situation expressed in the behaviouristic relationships of the community subject to certain constraints, for example the absence of unemployment. In this case the system would vary as if most of the old relationships of the community were still in operation, some would have to be scrapped to achieve the supposedly new objectives. On the other hand the government might ignore indications of past behaviour on the assumption that they knew best.

In the sort of mixed economy in which we live to-day the situation, still supposed ideal, lies somewhere between these two extremes. In many spheres the old behaviouristic relationships continue to exercise a determining influence on certain variables. Other variables, by legal measures and in other ways, are effectively put equal to a constant. The more the government believes in controls rather than in the old mechanism, the more, if they feel all is not well, will they tend to suppress some of the old relationships and replace them with new ones. The direct method will not always serve and in such cases the government will try to alter the parameters in the old behaviouristic relationships while leaving them in their old form. The present policy as regards saving is a mixture of these two approaches. Fiscal policy is intended to ensure among other things that government saving shall be equal to a certain constant while at the same time efforts are being made in various ways to encourage the community to increase their saving.

We thus reach a state of affairs in which certain relationships, the government's, are particularly liable to sudden change and in which conscious efforts are made to change the parameters in other relationships. If the government knew just what to expect from the community (and from nature and other outside influences) they could frustrate this behaviour where they thought such a course desirable and insert for certain variables the values they thought desirable. They would have to be careful how they did this since otherwise they might set up oscillations or one-sided movements, but in principle they could do it. The fact of the matter is, however, that in quantitative terms the government has at best a very vague idea of what to expect from the community and consequently cannot set its course and stick to it. When the community behaves normally but in a way that was not expected the government must change the system a little and they must keep on until by trial and error they have got things right. Even under ideal conditions this process of adjustment might take a long time and have many unforeseen consequences.

The ideal world which we have been assuming is one in which, given the constancy of the relationships of the system, we could predict its future movement exactly. Granted that in the sort of detail required this assumption of constancy is plausible, it would in fact be possible to make more or less exact predictions. But as I have said already we do not live in an ideal world. In fact we cannot write down exact equations; at best we can only determine each of the $(n-m)$ variables to within a probability distribution. There are additional degrees of freedom which we cannot absorb in exact equations and which we must leave to the control of chance. The repercussions of this obvious fact on the ideal situation is to enhance all the elements of uncertainty which lead to continual modification of plans.

This description of the prediction problem in economics, formal though it is, should be sufficient to bring home the formidable difficulties involved. The simplified model which I used to illustrate the minimum elements needed in making a full prediction presupposed an immense amount of knowledge. Its purpose, as will have been obvious from the sequel, was not to show that the problem was in principle easy if a certain line of approach were adopted, but to show the logical elements involved in a very simple case, elements which must be supplied by intuition or in some other way if they are not supplied by econometric studies. Indeed, the difficulties are so great that complete dynamic systems in quantitative form have rarely been developed. Tinbergen who has, I think, done more in this field than any other investigator, has been mainly concerned, in his published work* at any rate, with the autoregressive structure of economic systems and their policy implications rather than with actual predictions. More recently, however, Klein has worked out† models for the United States which he has used in making short-term predictions. There can be no doubt, in my view, that, difficult though it may be in practice, this is the right method to adopt. Clearly it is likely to be easier to apply in a comparatively free economy like the United States than in a partially controlled economy such as there is in this country. In fact it would appear‡ that Klein's model has given substantially better results than many of the static models that were used§ in the United States just after the war.

* See *An Econometric Approach to Business Cycle Problems* (1937), *Les Fondements Mathématiques de La Stabilisation du Mouvement des Affaires* (1938) and op. cit. (1939).

† See 'Economic Fluctuations in the United States 1921–1941' (second draft by L. R. Klein issued by the Cowles Commission in mimeographed form).

‡ See 'A Postmortem of Transition Predictions of National Product', by L. R. Klein, in the *Journal of Political Economy*, vol. LIV, no. 4 (August 1946), pp. 289–308.

§ See, for example, 'Forecasting Gross National Product and Employment During the Transition Period: an Example of the National Budget Method', by E. E. Hagen and N. Kirkpatrick, in *Studies in Income and Wealth*, vol. X (1947), pp. 94–109.

XIII. PREDICTION FROM STATIC MODELS

By way of conclusion let us take a glance at some of these static approaches. One method which has been used is to require only that certain accounting identities shall be fulfilled in forecasts of the entries in the social accounts. This condition imposes formal consistency on the predictions but nothing more. A step further is to require in addition that certain static behaviouristic relationships are fulfilled. An example of this approach which is only a slight over-simplification of methods which have actually been adopted may be set out thus.

As before, let X_1 = consumption, X_2 = asset formation and X_3 = income. Then we may write

$$X_1 = a + bX_3, \qquad (60)$$

$$X_3 = X_1 + X_2, \qquad (61)$$

$$X_2 = k. \qquad (62)$$

In this approach X_2, asset formation, is assumed to be exogenous, and its probable value in the prediction period is assessed independently of the model and put equal to a constant k. Equation (61) is the familiar accounting identity, income equals consumption plus asset formation, while equation (60) reflects the behaviour of consumers. If we substitute the right-hand sides of (60) and (62) for X_1 and X_2 in (61) and solve for X_3 we obtain

$$X_3 = \frac{a+k}{(1-b)}, \qquad (63)$$

whence

$$X_1 = \frac{a+bk}{(1-b)}. \qquad (64)$$

This line of approach may be refined in many ways. An example of such a refinement is the model given* by Kaldor with the object of analysing alternative fiscal policies for full employment. An essential element of all such models is the existence of certain variables which are fixed outside the model. In this way a static model can be made to say something about the future. Certain degrees of freedom are not absorbed by the model but are absorbed instead by guesses or estimates, made outside the model, of the future value of certain variables.

Kaldor's model was intended primarily to examine the implications of alternative routes to full employment rather than to make definite predictions for a closely specified period. This difference, however, is not important, for the question of whether a merely hypothetical or an

* See *Full Employment in a Free Society* (1944), by Lord Beveridge, appendix C by N. Kaldor, pp. 344–401. For an algebraic statement and brief examination of this model, see 'Economic Models with Special Reference to Mr Kaldor's System', by R. Stone and E. F. Jackson, in *The Economic Journal*, vol. LVI, no. 224 (December 1946), pp. 554–67. For a more extended critique of this type of model, see L. R. Klein, op. cit. (1946), and 'Model-Building and Fiscal Policy', by A. G. Hart, in *American Economic Review*, vol. XXXV, no. 4 (September 1945), pp. 531–58.

actually expected situation is being analysed by such a method depends on the nature of the estimates of the supposedly exogenous variables. It is important to keep this point in mind since in so far as this particular model turned out to give an over-optimistic picture of the post-war situation the reason is mainly to be found in the over-optimistic assumptions about the variables treated as exogenous, such as the national income, and not in the econometric methods themselves. On the other hand, without some such approach as Kaldor employed, it would not have been possible to trace the repercussions of alternative fiscal policies.

SOME ILLUSTRATIONS OF THE PROBLEMS
OF MEASUREMENT

XIV. SOCIAL ACCOUNTING

In this and the following sections I shall examine the problems of definition, measurement and collection that arise in the field of national income and expenditure or, as I think it is better called, social accounting.* As I mentioned in Section IV the characteristics of an economic system met with in this branch of economic inquiry provide a good example of the problems involved in handling empirical constructs. I shall also hope to show that the elements of a social accounting system are of special interest since they clearly exhibit a formal structure and are not simply a set of isolated concepts. For this reason they exemplify the necessity for economic and statistical design about which I have already spoken.

Social accounting, which will be familiar to most of you from the national income White Papers, is intended to classify, measure and present the transactions which take place over a period in an economic system in such a way that as far as possible they will accord with economic definitions and distinctions and as a result will be useful for economic analysis especially as it relates to practical economic policy. The definitions we adopt, the facts we need to collect and the classification which we impose on them are not by any means given in nature but at the same time they cannot, if they are to be usable, be developed regardless of the nature of the actual world.

Thus under the general heading of economic design I shall look at the problems of social accounting first from an economic point of view and second from an accounting point of view. The first will direct us on to the question of what we are trying to do while the second will force us to attend carefully to questions of consistency and of practical methods of doing it.

XV. THE THREE FORMS OF ECONOMIC ACTIVITY

From the economic point of view we can take as our point of departure the three primary concepts of production, consumption and adding to wealth. By production we mean bringing into being goods and services (or perhaps more strictly the utilities associated with these) on which

* For a more detailed discussion of many of the problems that arise in this field, see 'Definition and Measurement of the National Income and Related Totals', by the present writer, appended to *Measurement of National Income and the Construction of Social Accounts* (1947), which was the report of the sub-committee on National Income Statistics of the League of Nations Committee of Statistical Experts. See also my 'Functions and Criteria of a System of Social Accounting' to be published in the volume of papers arising out of the Cambridge meeting of the International Association for Research in Income and Wealth held in September 1949.

members of the community or the community as a whole through its agents set a valuation. By consumption we mean using up and wearing out the fruits of production and by adding to wealth we mean preserving the fruits of production for the purpose of contributing to consumption at a later date.

The relationship between these basic concepts can conveniently be illustrated by means of the Keynesian identities in their simplest form. Let us write

Y = Income or Product,

C = Consumption,

S = Saving,

I = Asset Formation (or Investment).

These variables are related by two independent relationships

$$Y \equiv C + S,$$
$$S \equiv I.$$

These relationships are illustrated in the following diagram in which the three aspects of economic activity, production, consumption and adding to wealth, are represented by the three boxes bearing these names, and in which the basic variables are represented as flows between these boxes.

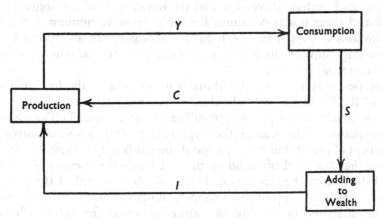

DIAGRAM 2. Relationships between Production, Consumption and Adding to Wealth

There are several points that arise even from this elementary example.

In the first place the economy depicted is naturally closed; there is no 'abroad' or 'rest of the world' with which it has economic relationships.

In the second place, as can be seen by comparing the diagram with the two identities, the sum of the flows at each box or node in the diagram is zero. The form of activity production has two flows coming in, representing respectively the proceeds from the provision of goods and services for consumption and goods and services for adding to wealth, and these proceeds are exhausted by income payments to the form of activity consumption, which receives the gain from the contributions of labour, capital and other factors of production engaged in the productive process. This income which flows in as revenue to the form of activity consumption is partly spent, as we have already seen, on goods and services provided by the form of activity production while the remainder is saved and transferred to the form of activity adding to wealth, at which point it is converted into real assets (hence the term 'asset formation') provided by the form of activity production. This description of the three basic forms of activity suggests that the boxes in the diagram may be regarded as accounts which balance in the ordinary way. This is in fact the case and I shall explain the precise nature of these accounts when we come to the problem of accounting design.

In the third place, while the general nature of the three basic forms of activity may be fairly clear from this brief description, it is evident that for practical purposes we must specify what payments for services we are going to route from producers through consumers, and what distinction we are going to adopt between purchases by consumers out of income and purchases coming under the heading of asset formation made out of saving. If I had stressed the accounting viewpoint at the beginning, which might in some ways have been the simplest thing to do, I should perhaps have obscured the importance of a searching discussion of these questions, since, for the purpose of business accounts, conventions have already been fully elaborated. In many cases the accounting conventions are also satisfactory to the economist, but in other cases this is not so.

The best way to proceed I think is to go back to the fundamental idea of the income of an individual as the maximum value which he can consume during a period and still expect to be as well off at the end of the period as he was at the beginning.* This definition involves a concept of maintaining one's capital since it is only if capital is maintained that the level of spending has not made the spender worse off (or, if his capital has increased, better off) by the end of the period. Thus, for example, if profit is a component of income it is necessary that this profit should be the true operating surplus of the period after all internal provisions, e.g. for depreciation, have been deducted as a business expense. If this is not done the resulting 'gross' profit cannot all be spent on consumption goods and services without entailing a failure to maintain capital.

This term capital is perhaps ambiguous since it is ordinarily used by accountants and business men to mean the contribution of the proprietors to an enterprise which would normally be contributed in money though it may be contributed in kind. In talking about maintaining capital intact, however, the economist is thinking of the capacity

* See *Value and Capital* (1939), by J. R. Hicks, ch. XIV, p. 172.

and facilities available for production, i.e. he is thinking of the real assets of the concern, whether these are in the form of fixed assets or of inventories. From the economic point of view the provision for maintaining capital intact must aim at enabling these facilities to be maintained without resort to additional borrowing, so that in times of sharply rising prices the accounting convention to provide for depreciation on the basis of original cost would almost certainly not form an adequate provision from the economic point of view. The only case in which such a provision could be regarded as adequate would be if the market value of the investments, in which the depreciation fund was kept, had been rising in step with the rise in the price of the assets to be replaced. This is a good example of a case in which the ideas of economists and the majority of practising accountants tend to differ. The other main point of difference is over the question of the valuation of inventories. In both these cases I believe the difference of view can largely be traced to two circumstances, first that the accountant is more concerned than the economist with questions of individual proprietorship, and second that many accounting conventions that flourish to-day were developed in a period in which prices either were, or at least were generally thought to be, reasonably stable. Under a régime in which stable prices are the norm the economic and accounting treatment of these difficult subjects would not be very different from one another.

The need to distinguish between production costs which do and do not form part of income arises of course equally in the case of labour income. In some industries for example it is usual to require employees to buy certain working tools and equipment out of their wages. In such a case we should clearly not include the whole of wages as paid in the income flow but only that part which is available after the cost of tools and equipment has been met. If we do not do this we should get into income sums which could not be freely spent if the assets employed in production are to be maintained.

The converse case arises where amenities are provided at a place of work, for example air-conditioning, rest rooms, pit-head baths and the like. These amenities undoubtedly represent a gain to the employees and we might wish therefore to attempt to include them in income; but in practice it is hardly possible to decide in such cases what part of the expense incurred by the employer is in excess of unavoidable costs of production and no attempt therefore is made to include any part of them in the income stream.

Yet another example arises in cases where employers provide working clothing for their employees. This clothing may be of two kinds: first it may take the form of helmets, heavy gloves or visors, which are needed in addition to the ordinary clothing for the performance of particular tasks. The second is exemplified by uniforms which are substitutes for ordinary clothing during the time that the employee is engaged in his work. On the principles given above the first kind of clothing should be excluded since it is purely an additional cost of the work performed by

the employee and the provision of it does not release any of his pur-
chasing power for other purposes. There is, however, a good case for
including the second class since the provision of uniforms means that
the income which the employees have to spend on ordinary clothing
can be reduced to what is necessary for their leisure hours.

From these examples it will be evident that it is not easy to draw up
an exact and comprehensive statement of the distinction between income payments and other costs of production. The general idea is that
the former comprise all net sums, actual or imputed, which add to the
freely disposable gain of the recipient. They are the return for his contribution to production by way either of labour or capital.

Fourth, we have been discussing so far the treatment of the flows in
the very simplified example between the form of activity production
and the form of activity consumption. Let us now turn to the flows
between the form of activity consumption and the form of activity
adding to wealth. In order to decide on the meaning of saving, which
is the excess of income over consumption expenditure, we have to
decide on the meaning of the latter. The guiding idea in this case is that
consumption expenditure comprises that expenditure the benefit from
which is fully taken up in the period of account. Thus expenditure on
rent or on the hire of the services of equipment such as cookers or water-
heaters is clearly consumption expenditure, and so, if we are considering
an accounting period as long as one year, is the expenditure on perish-
able food, since the inventory change over so long a period is negligible.
In the case of durable consumers' goods on the other hand, such as
clothing, motor-cars, domestic equipment, etc., the gain from a purchase in one year clearly extends to future years when the durable goods
will still be in existence and will be yielding a flow of utilities to their
possessors. Accordingly from many points of view we should like to
regard expenditure on such items as asset formation made out of saving.
In fact, however, we do not do this and it is the usual practice of
national income statisticians to restrict the capital expenditure of
individuals to purchases of land and buildings and to regard expenditure
on all other durable consumers' goods as current expenditure which is
written off in the year in which it is made. The reason for this is a practical one, namely that consumers do not usually regard their households
as business enterprises employing durable equipment which is to be
depreciated, and do not either provide for the depreciation of durable
goods in the vast majority of cases or compute the gain to the household
arising from the ownership of durable goods.

The result of this convention is to introduce a line of demarcation
between current and capital expenditure which in the case of consumers is different from and less satisfactory than that adopted in the
case of enterprises. The main effect, however, is not on the level of
aggregate production or income but on the way in which we regard this
total as being distributed between consumption and adding to wealth.
The measures of income and product which flow from this treatment of

consumers' durable goods will be less than those which would arise if we treated consumers' durable goods in the same way as the durable goods of enterprises by the amount of the imputed net gain to consumers from possessing their durable goods. It is probable that this amount would neither be large nor variable and certainly it could not be estimated with any accuracy. Consequently, for practical purposes, our concepts of income and product will not suffer materially from this omission. On the other hand, over the course of time, when on the whole we may assume that the total stock of consumers' durable goods is on the increase, we shall get the impression that consumption is somewhat higher and additions to wealth somewhat lower than is actually the case; for example the increase of two million or so in the number of motor-cars in the hands of consumers between 1900 and 1940 will have appeared at one time or another as a part of consumers' current expenditure and not as a part of their capital expenditure, so that a balance sheet for consumers drawn up in accordance with these principles would not reflect the increase in the stock of privately owned motor-cars since they would all have been written off at the time they were purchased.

XVI. TRANSACTIONS IN THE BRITISH ECONOMY IN 1948: AN EXAMPLE

So far I have only indicated the basic structure of economic activity by means of a very simple example. I shall now turn to an actual case illustrated by the transactions taking place in the British economy in 1948 as indicated in the official statistics.* The first thing to notice is that the British economy is not naturally closed and since we want a representation of transactions with no loose ends we must close it artificially by including a fourth box which we may label 'the rest of the world'. The second important point is that we now have to face various different means of organizing production and consumption and in particular the distinction between the private sector of the economy and public authorities. This last distinction does not add anything new from the standpoint of our three basic forms of economic activity. As I shall hope to show when I come to discuss the accounting aspect of these problems, everything fits neatly into its place, but for the time being it will be convenient if the incomings and outgoings of public authorities, in the provision and organization of common services such as defence, justice, education and public health, are thought of as consolidated in the consumption box, being in fact nothing more than agency activities for the body of consumers as a whole.

With these provisos we may now add a fourth box to the simple diagram that appears on page 39 and show the minimum amount of additional detail which has to be added to my former diagram to make

* *National Income and Expenditure of the United Kingdom 1946 to 1948* (Cmd. 7649), H.M.S.O., April 1949.

it capable of representing the transactions of a typical economic system of the modern world.*

Let us start off by considering the income flows into the production sector, out of which the production costs are financed and any profit accruing from productive operations arises. We already have two such flows marked in the diagram. I will now rename them current expenditure at home, which in 1948 was £9,455 m., and capital expenditure on real assets, which was £2,334 m., and represents gross asset formation,

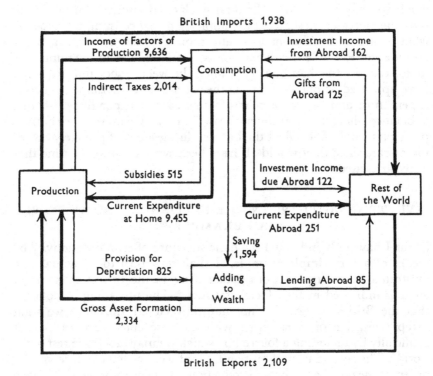

DIAGRAM 3. Transactions in the British Economy in 1948

that is to say asset formation before any provision has been made for the depreciation of existing fixed capital equipment and inventories. A further source of revenue from the sale of the output of British productive activity consists in sales to the rest of the world, i.e British exports of goods and services which amounted to £2,109 m. Over and

* A number of other forms of diagram representing systems of transactions have appeared in recent years but most of them are more elaborate than the one given here. See for example: *A System of National Book-keeping Illustrated by the Experience of the Netherlands Economy* (1946), by J. B. D. Derksen, being Occasional Paper X of the National Institute of Economic and Social Research, London; *A System of Concepts Describing the Economic Circulation and Production Process* (1948, mimeographed), by O. Aukrust, P. J. Bjerve and R. Frisch; and 'The Diagrammatic Representation of National Income Flows', by R. C. Tress, in *Economica*, n.s., vol. xv, no. 60 (November 1948), pp. 276–88.

THE BRITISH ECONOMY IN 1948

above all these sales proceeds, production also received assistance from
the government in the form of subsidies, which can be represented by
a flow from consumption to production and amounted to £515 m.
The thin lines in the diagram indicate the fact that it is a unilateral
payment. In the other cases we have considered so far, the sums
accruing to the form of activity production have been in respect of
goods and services provided. In this case, however, the subsidy payment is made, not in respect of goods and services provided, but simply
to enable producers to sell their goods and services to consumers at less
than their cost of production.

These four sources of revenue exhaust those which are available to
the form of activity production. There will of course be an enormous
number of transactions between British enterprises, but these will all disappear when the transactions of British enterprises are consolidated, as
they are in this representation. We could if we liked indicate a flow
going from the production box and returning to it, but here we are only
considering the flows between different forms of economic activity.

On the outgoing side the form of activity production has to meet
a number of costs. In the case of any individual firm a large part of these
costs is likely to arise in the purchase of materials and services from
other firms, but these will all disappear by consolidation in the present
example and we shall be left with the purchases of goods and services
from the rest of the world, i.e. British imports, which amounted to
£1,938 m. Another cost of production which we must take into account
is the provision for depreciation, which amounted to £825 m. and which
I have indicated by a unilateral flow of funds from production to adding
to wealth. There is also a similar unilateral flow of funds from production to consumption in respect of indirect taxes, which amounted
to £2,014 m. As I have said, public authorities engaged in organizing
common services are consolidated in this representation with private consumers under the form of activity consumption and these indirect taxes,
which are a cost of business operations, accrue to them as a form of incoming. Finally, there is a second flow from production to consumption
in respect of the services contributed by the factors of production, which
amounted to £9,636 m. This is the flow which we previously called
income and represents the sum of the income payments of all forms,
wages, salaries, profit, interest and net rents, arising out of British production. We can now see that the production sector is in balance, with
its operating incomings equal to its operating outgoings.

Let us now turn to the form of activity consumption. We have seen
so far that there are two forms of incoming, income of the factors of
production and indirect taxes. There is also another form of incoming
in so far as this country lends money abroad and receives investment
income in respect of it. This investment income, which is represented
by a thin flow from the rest of the world to consumption, amounted
to £162 m. But this was a gross flow and in 1948 there was also a flow
of investment income in the opposite direction amounting to £122 m.

which was due from this country to the rest of the world in respect of foreign investments in the United Kingdom. In addition there was a further incoming flow of £125 m. in respect of gifts from abroad under the E.R.P. programme and also a further outgoing in respect of consumption expenditure abroad amounting to £251 m. which represented expenditure by British tourists and also by the British government in discharging its obligations abroad. Finally, since we have now taken into account all the transactions between consumption on the one hand and production and the rest of the world on the other, there remains only the balance in the consumption account which is transferred to the form of activity adding to wealth and which, as in the previous example, is termed saving. This balance was positive in 1948 and amounted to £1,594 m.

This leaves us with only one more form of activity to consider: when we have filled in all the flows into or out of production, consumption and adding to wealth, we shall automatically have completed the whole picture, since the rest of the world only represents the other end of those flows which are external to the British economy. In fact we have only one more flow to put into the picture, and this arises from the fact that in 1948 there was a favourable balance on the current account of the United Kingdom with the rest of the world accompanied by a corresponding amount of lending from the former to the latter. This sum is shown as a unilateral flow from the form of activity adding to wealth into the rest of the world and amounted to £85 m. It may be seen with this final addition that the four boxes are in balance in the sense that the flows in are exactly equal to the flows out.

This last flow representing net lending abroad is shown as a flow out of the form of activity adding to wealth since the benefit from lending or borrowing is likely to extend beyond a single year. It must not, of course, be assumed from this that there is any meaning to be attached to the idea that the lending or borrowing in some specific sense is used for capital purposes. It may perfectly well happen that the object of borrowing by one country is not to increase capital expenditure in that country but to make available a larger flow of consumption goods there. If, for example, as happened in the immediate post-war years, the British economy borrowed x for the purpose of importing more consumption goods to the value of x the net result on the system of flows might be to increase British imports by x (thus putting the account of the rest of the world in balance), to increase gross expenditure at home by x (thus putting the production account in balance), and to reduce British saving by x (thus putting the consumption account and the account of adding to wealth in balance). In other words, the object of a given amount of borrowing might be to make possible a given volume of capital expenditure with a smaller amount of British saving and a larger amount of saving abroad, which was diverted to the advantage of the British economy.

XVII. THE DERIVATION OF THE EXAMPLE FROM PUBLISHED SOURCES

The transactions of the British economy in 1948 depicted in Diagram 3 may be set out in accounting form.

TABLE 2. SIMPLIFIED ACCOUNTING SYSTEM, SHOWING THE TRANSACTIONS IN THE BRITISH ECONOMY IN 1948

PRODUCTION (£ million)

Payable		*Receivable*	
1. Purchases from overseas (33)	1,938	6. Sales to satisfy consumption needs (11)	9,455
2. Indirect taxes (18)	2,014		
3. Provision for depreciation (25)	825	7. Sales of fixed assets and value of additions to inventories (22)	2,334
4. Sums due to factors of production including trading profit (17)	9,636	8. Sales abroad (28)	2,109
		9. Subsidies (13)	515
5. Total	14,413	10. Total	14,413

CONSUMPTION (£ million)

Payable		*Receivable*	
11. Current expenditure at home (6)	9,455	17. Sums due from production to factors of production (4)	9,636
12. Current expenditure abroad (34)	251	18. Indirect taxes (2)	2,014
13. Subsidies (9)	515	19. Investment income from abroad (29)	162
14. Investment income due from abroad (35)	122	20. Gifts from abroad (30)	125
15. Saving (26)	1,594		
16. Total	11,937	21. Total	11,937

ADDING TO WEALTH (£ million)

Payable		*Receivable*	
22. Purchases of fixed assets and value of additions to inventories (7)	2,334	25. Provision for depreciation (3)	825
		26. Saving (15)	1,594
23. Lending abroad (31)	85		
24. Total	2,419	27. Total	2,419

REST OF THE WORLD (£ million)

Payable		*Receivable*	
28. Purchases from the United Kingdom (8)	2,109	33. Sales to British production (1)	1,938
29. Investment income due to the United Kingdom (19)	162	34. Sales to British consumption (12)	251
30. Gifts to the United Kingdom (20)	125	35. Investment income due from the United Kingdom (14)	122
31. Lending to the United Kingdom (23)	−85		
32. Total	2,311	36. Total	2,311

These figures may be found in many places in Cmd. 7649. Most of them appear in table 2 on p. 6 to which reference is made below wherever possible.

1. Table $2.5(a+b+c)$.

2. Table 2.10 *less* table 25.2. Following the usage adopted by the United Nations, employers' contributions to social security are treated not as indirect taxes but as supplements to wages and salaries. Here they are included in item 4 below.

3. Table $13.4+8$.

4. Table 4.10 *plus* table 25.2 *less* £150 m. estimated (Cmd. 7649, p. 17) to be that part of the change in the value of inventories due entirely to price increases and here excluded from income.

6. Table $2.1(a+b)+2(a+b+c)$ *less* £212 m. estimated to be the value of sales of surplus stores (£257 m.: see table $2.3(c)$) other than equipment sold to the Government of India (£45 m.: see note to item 46 of table 24 on p. 58). The £212 m. of proceeds from the sales of surplus stores are thus treated here as an offset to current expenditure. These stores were not treated as an addition to inventories when they were acquired and so are not allowed to diminish inventories when they are sold. The £45 millions of proceeds from the sales to the Government of India are here treated as a reduction of British claims on the rest of the world.

7. Table $2.3(a+b)$ *less* £150 m. The deduction is needed (see note to item 4 above) since inventory formation is measured here by the value of the physical change in inventories and not by the change in their money value.

8. Table $2.3(d)+4(a+b+c+d+e)$ *less* £45 m. in respect of sales to the Government of India (see note to item 6 above).

9. Table 2.9.

12. Table $2.1(c)+2(d)$.

14. Table 19.50.

15. Table $18.41+42+44$ *plus* £212 m. in respect of sales of surplus stores here treated as an offset to government current expenditure *less* £150 m. in respect of the inventory revaluation adjustment (see note to item 4 above) here treated as a reduction of profits and therefore of saving *plus* £125 m. estimated to be the gift (as opposed to loan) element of the E.R.P. grant received by this country. This gift is here treated as a current incoming and therefore adds to British saving as defined here.

19. Table 19.53.

23. Table $2.3(d)+4+5+7$ *plus* £125 m. in respect of the gift element of the E.R.P. grant here treated as a current incoming and not as an element of borrowing *less* £45 m. in respect of the sales to the Government of India here treated as a decrease in British claims on the rest of the world.

XVIII. THE STRUCTURE OF TRANSACTIONS AND SOME IMPORTANT NATIONAL AGGREGATES

I have emphasized from the outset that the main interest in this field lies in the presentation of the structure of transactions, and the simplest form of this structure which I believe brings out all the essential features, but avoids unnecessary complications, is contained in Diagram 3. Let us now consider the relationship between this structure and such familiar aggregates of transactions as the national income, the gross national product and the like.

The flow from production to consumption, £9,636 m., represents the income of the factors of production arising from services contributed to British enterprises, enterprises being understood in this context in a broad sense to include individuals working on their own account, landlords, professional persons and those who render individual services. This total may conveniently be termed the domestic product, since it represents the net value of production taking place within the limits of the United Kingdom. The national income is usually defined as the income accruing to the factors of production normally resident in or owned by persons normally resident in the United Kingdom independently of whether their contribution to production is made in this country or abroad. Consequently in order to get the national income we must add to the domestic product the net income from overseas investment, which was £40 m. in 1948, giving a total of £9,676 m. for the national income.

Let us now return to the net domestic product and see how this is generated in terms of different forms of expenditure. The position may be set out as follows:

	£ million
Net domestic product	9,636
Consumption at home	9,455
Net asset formation at home	1,509
Net exports of goods and services	171
Less net indirect taxes	−1,499
	9,636

There is no difficulty in seeing that consumption expenditure at home will contribute to the incomes which can be paid out by British enterprises. The same is true of asset formation at home except that here it may not be immediately obvious why the figure is shown on a net basis. The reason is that the difference between gross and net asset formation, namely provision for depreciation, forms a part of the costs of operating activities which cannot get passed on to the factors of production. As we saw at an earlier stage, when we were discussing the concept of income, the element of profit in total income has to be taken after provision for depreciation has been made. Consequently, like any other cost which does not appear as a part of the income of the factors of production, it must be excluded from the expenditure side of the statement. Of course it is not essential that it should be deducted simply from asset formation. We can, if we like, think of asset formation as entered gross and the total of provision for depreciation deducted from the selling value of consumption at home, asset formation at home and British exports into the cost of which it enters. I shall not attempt to give an alternative classification on this basis since the information needed is not provided.

The inclusion of net exports of goods and services is quite straightforward. Purchases of British exports contribute to the incomings of British production out of which income payments are made, while the imports must be deducted as a charge on these incomings. Looking at the matter in this way we can see that the value of British imports will be reflected either in consumption at home or in asset formation at home or in British exports, and any part of these totals which represents expenditure on imports cannot be available for paying the incomes of the British factors of production. The final item shows the deduction of net indirect taxes from the other items to reach a total equal to the net domestic product. This is needed since indirect taxes form part of the value of the different forms of expenditure listed, which again are a prior charge on production and are not available for the payment of incomes to the factors of production. Subsidies may be regarded as negative indirect taxes and they have to be added since they form a source of revenue for production but are not included in the value of the different forms of expenditure.

Having set the table out in this way, it will doubtless have been perceived that all we have done is to rearrange the transactions flowing into or out of the form of activity production. The outgoing payment income of the factors of production is balanced in this rearrangement by the incoming flow current expenditure at home plus the net incoming flow net asset formation at home plus the net incoming flow net exports of goods and services minus the net outgoing flow net indirect taxes. Thus the national income, or rather that part of it which arises from British production, which I have called the net domestic product, and the corresponding expenditure concept, are obtained simply by a rearrangement of the transactions entering and leaving the form of activity production. It is for this reason that it is regarded by economists as an important concept in describing the state of the economic system.

We have already seen that the national income is equal to the payments to the factors of production (£9,636 m.) plus net income from overseas investments (£40 m.) and we will now consider the expenditure concept which corresponds to this concept of income. In the first place we must add current expenditure abroad (£251 m.) and net gifts abroad (−£125 m.) to current expenditure at home (£9,455 m.) giving a total for consumption expenditure of £9,581 m. Net asset formation at home (£1,509 m.) and the adjustment for net indirect taxes (−£1,499 m.) remain as before and the final concept we have to introduce relates to transactions with the rest of the world. We start with net exports of goods and services (£171 m.) and we must add to this net income from overseas investments (£40 m.) and net gifts from the rest of the world (£125 m.) and we must deduct current expenditure abroad (£251 m.) making a total of £85 m., i.e. the balance of expenditure on current account, which is exactly equal to the net lending to the rest of the world. Thus if we take the total of current expenditure (£9,581 m.) and add the net increase in wealth comprising net asset formation at home (£1,509 m.) plus net lending abroad (£85 m.) or £1,594 m. in all, and if we make the adjustment already explained for net indirect taxes, we reach an expenditure total equal to the national income. In other words the national income is the sum of current expenditures (including net gifts abroad) and of additions to wealth adjusted, by the correction for net indirect taxes, to the basis of valuation adopted in measuring the national product by taking the sum of payments to factors of production. It and the corresponding expenditure concept can be obtained by first consolidating the forms of activity consumption and adding to wealth and then rearranging the incoming and outgoing flows.

At this point we may mention the fact already obvious from the diagram that if we take the sum of net asset formation at home plus net lending abroad ($£1,509$ m. $+£85$ m. $=£1,594$ m.) we reach a figure of the total saving of the community. This is obvious from a rearrangement of the flows entering and leaving the form of activity adding to wealth.

So far we have mainly concentrated on the net domestic product and on the national income. Let us see now how these concepts are related to the gross national product, the third aggregate product concept which is largely used in economic analysis. We may start off with the net domestic product ($£9,636$ m.), which it will be remembered is valued at factor cost and to which we may add net indirect taxes ($£1,499$ m.) giving a total of $£11,135$ m. To this total of the net domestic product valued at market prices we may add net income from overseas investments ($£40$ m.) giving an overall total of $£11,175$ m. This total may be called the net national product at market prices and differs from the national income simply by the inclusion of net indirect taxes ($£1,499$ m.) The expenditure side of the account will be exactly the same as the net national expenditure ($£9,676$ m.) already dealt with except for the fact that the deduction of net indirect taxes is not made. Accordingly it will comprise current expenditure at home and abroad ($£9,581$ m.) plus net asset formation at home ($£1,509$ m.) plus net lending abroad ($£85$ m.). As we have already seen the sum of the last two items ($£1,594$ m.) is equal to national saving. And so we can see that the net national product at market prices is equal to the sum of current expenditure at market prices plus saving of all sectors of the economy. If now we add provision for depreciation ($£825$ m.) to both sides of the account we obtain on the product side the gross national product as the term is used in the United States, and on the expenditure side the sum of current expenditure at home and abroad ($£9,581$ m.) plus gross asset formation at home ($£2,334$ m.) plus net lending abroad ($£85$ m.). The sum of the last two items ($£2,419$ m.) represents the gross additions to wealth made in 1948 and consequently the gross national product is equal to the sum of consumption expenditures and gross additions to wealth.

XIX. THE GROUP STRUCTURE OF TRANSACTIONS*

The diagrams I have been using to explain the interrelations of transactions in the national economy are simply network diagrams in which the different forms of economic activity are nodes and the transactions are represented by directed branches passing from one node to another. The only formal property of such a system is that the sum of the flows at any node is equal to zero, which expresses the fact that each of the

* For a further discussion of this and other properties of systems of transactions, see the present writer's 'Social Accounting, Aggregation and Invariance', in *Cahiers du Congrès International de Comptabilité* (1948) and reprinted (in French), in *Economie Appliquée*, tome II, no. 1 (January–March 1949), pp. 26–54.

forms of activity is in balance. In a system of four nodes such as the one
I have just been describing we have already seen that one is dependent
on the rest, that is to say when all the connexions have been made with
the other three all the connexions of the fourth have been made as well.
Consequently such a system places three constraints on the joint variation of all the transactions. In my example there were thirteen distinct
transactions, three of which may in suitable circumstances all be determined from a knowledge of the remainder, since the three constraints,
which are simply definitional equations connecting the transactions,
may be used to eliminate three transactions out of the thirteen. Evidently
if we had n nodes in the complete system the number of constraints
would be $(n-1)$.

The formal property that the sum of the flows at any node is zero
gives rise to the group structure of a system of transactions. To illustrate
this let us go back to the first example of two relationships connecting
income, consumption, saving and asset formation, and let us redraw
Diagram 2 in a form which is more suitable to the present application.
It will then appear as follows:

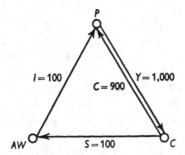

DIAGRAM 4. Alternative Presentation of Diagram 2

In this system we may form an aggregate of transactions equal to the
sum of the flows out of the form of activity consumption and into the
form of activity adding to wealth. This aggregate will be equal to
national outlay, i.e. the sum of consumption expenditure and saving
(since in this example the flow from the form of activity production to
the form of activity adding to wealth is zero). It will appear as the left-
hand member of the following diagram:

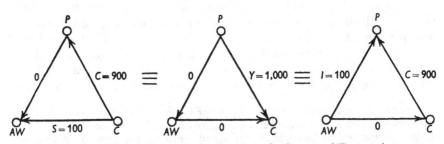

DIAGRAM 5. Illustration of Group Property of a System of Transactions

It will be observed that since this aggregate of transactions contains all the flows out of the form of activity consumption and this total is equal to the sum of the flows into the form of activity consumption, we may obtain an identical total of transactions by reversing the flows at the consumption node, while keeping the other flow the same. The result of this operation is shown in the middle diagram, from which it will be seen that the resulting total of transactions is simply the national income. In this case, however, we have all the flows coming out of the form of activity production and consequently we may obtain another total of transactions identically equal to the former totals by changing the direction of the flows at this point while keeping the other flows the same. The result of this operation is shown in the right-hand diagram which comprises the sum of consumption expenditure and asset formation which are both flows into the production node. In this right-hand diagram we have all the flows going out of the form of activity adding to wealth and consequently we might think that we could generate another total by reversing the flows at this node. This, indeed, we can do but the resulting total of transactions will not be a new one, but simply the national outlay shown in the left-hand diagram. The three totals of transactions that we have already generated by the process of a change in direction of the flows at one of the nodes form a group in which the elements are the transactions entering or leaving a given node, and the group operation is the operation of changing the direction of all the flows at a node at which we have all the flows pointing in one direction. Continuous transformations of this kind will simply lead back to members of the group which have already occurred. The application of the group operation gives rise to a group of identical aggregates of transactions which corresponds to the single-cycle permutation group. The group of all permutations of n symbols is called the symmetric group of degree n and contains $(n)!$ permutations of which $(n-1)!$ are single-cycle permutations. Thus with n accounts there are $(n-1)!$ groups of connected sets of flows of the type described, no member of any one of which can be transformed into a member of any other by the group operation of substitution. Each of the $(n-1)!$ groups contains n members. It is from this group property of systems of transactions that the possibility of deriving aggregates equal in value to other aggregates arises.*

XX. SYSTEMS OF TRANSACTIONS FROM THE VIEWPOINT OF ACCOUNTANCY

In setting out to explain the structure of a system of transactions I took as my point of departure the primitive economic concepts of production, consumption and adding to wealth. We may think of production, to

* For a fuller treatment of the number of equivalents to an aggregate of transactions, see a forthcoming article with this title by J. Durbin to appear in *Economie Appliquée*.

take an example, as mainly centred in business enterprises, but it is clear that not all the transactions of business enterprises will appear in the form of activity production in my system. For example, business enterprises will very frequently save something out of their income, and as we have seen all the saving in the system is represented by a flow from the form of activity consumption to the form of activity adding to wealth. In a similar way we may think of the form of activity consumption as mainly taking place in households, but again households may acquire assets, e.g. a family may purchase a new house and as we have seen all expenditure of this kind takes place between the form of activity adding to wealth and the form of activity production. Consequently we cannot identify the three basic forms of economic activity with any particular entities in the economic system, and accordingly the question arises: Is there anything else with which we can identify them? I shall now try to show that the three basic forms of economic activity are isomorphic with the three basic statements of an orthodox accounting structure.

An accounting structure for a business enterprise may be said to consist of a profit and loss account and a balance sheet. The profit and loss account may be subdivided into an operating section and a non-operating section, while we may form a third account by taking the differences in the entries between the balance sheets at the beginning and end of the period. I shall now try to demonstrate two things: first, that the transactions entering into the three forms of economic activity, production, consumption and adding to wealth, are isomorphic respectively with those appearing in the operating section of a profit and loss account, the non-operating section and an account summarizing the capital incomings and outgoings of the period, which in consolidated form would show the balance sheet differences over the period and which I shall call a resting account. Secondly, I shall demonstrate that this structure is fundamental to all entities and is in no way special to business enterprises. If we set up such a structure for all entities in the economy and consolidate not all the accounts for each type of entity but each type of account for all entities, we shall obtain a representation of the structure of transactions isomorphic with the one I have given earlier in terms of the three basic forms of economic activity.

If we go back to the form of activity production it will be seen that there are brought together at this point in the system all transactions connected with business operating activity. The incoming items were in the form of sales proceeds of different kinds and subsidies received from the government, while the outgoings were in respect of different sorts of cost such as imported goods, provision for depreciation, indirect taxes and income payments of wages, salaries, etc. From an accounting point of view the balance on this operating account is simply the operating profit which, in the system I have been discussing, appeared as part of the income of factors of production. So far as business enterprises are concerned this is a perfectly natural way of looking at the matter, but we must note that an exactly similar account may be set up for the provision of any service, e.g. the services of labour, and consolidated with business operating accounts to make up the form of activity production. If the labour is employed in an enterprise we may set up the operating account for labour in the following form. On the incoming side we have total sums due from the employing enterprise in respect of the labour provided, i.e. sales proceeds in providing labour services; and on the outgoing side we have any costs incurred in the provision of these services, such as tools to be purchased out of wages and a net balance which we may call income from wages, or the operating profit of providing labour services. If this operating account is now consolidated with the operating account for the enterprise employing the labour, then it will be seen that the wages paid appearing on the outgoing side of the enterprise operating account will cancel out with the sums receivable on the incoming side of the labour operating account, and the net result will be that the consolidated form will be identical with the original operating account for the employing enterprise.

This position will not arise, however, if the labour services are being provided not to an enterprise but direct to a household or government department. In this case the consolidation of a labour operating account with the operating accounts of enterprises will add something to both sides of the account, namely on the receivable side the sales proceeds from providing this type of labour service and on the outgoing side any expenses together with the income from wages. Thus, if our form of economic activity is to be all-inclusive and represent the transactions in respect of the provision for all forms of goods and services, including for example the direct services of labour, it is necessary to set up operating accounts for employees in which are entered the transactions connected with the services that they supply and to consolidate these operating accounts with the ordinary operating accounts of enterprises. This in fact has been done in the numerical example already given.

If we pass now to the form of activity consumption, it is natural to think of this in terms of the income and expenditure account of individual households. Just as the balance on the production account represented an operating profit, so the balance on the consumption account will represent some form of saving. In fact the account brings together non-operating current transactions and therefore we need to consolidate not only the income and expenditure accounts of individuals but also the non-operating accounts of enterprises, and the income and expenditure accounts of bodies, whether private or governmental, which are engaged in organizing the provision of final services for the community. The non-operating accounts of enterprises will show on their incoming side the profit from operations brought down from the operating account, together with certain net incomings mainly of a financial nature which form part of the income of the concern, and these sums will be distributed between taxes, dividends and withdrawals, and saving. In the case of institutions engaged in organizing common services for the community, it is quite clear that, in so far as these are private bodies not operating for profit, they can rightly be regarded as a simple extension of individual households to areas in which the services provided are not such as are capable of being organized on an individual basis. Charitable organizations, clubs and societies of all kinds, are all examples of this type of extension. The contributions of all these voluntary bodies to production will appear in the operating accounts of the factors of production which they employ and which, as we have already seen, will be consolidated, as in the case of domestic servants rendering direct services to households, with the operating accounts of business enterprises. This is in accordance with common sense since we do not think of these voluntary bodies as making profits or losses, but as either saving or dissaving over a period.

Now it is convenient to think of by far the greater part of the activities of public authorities as being concerned with the organization of common services in just the same way. When the central government organizes defence in war-time and incurs a large deficit on current account we do not think of the government as providing defence services at a loss. We merely think that over the period they have had to dissave in order to provide these services. As in the case of voluntary bodies, the contribution of the government to production will be reflected in the operating accounts of the factors of production which it employs. Accordingly we may identify the form of economic activity consumption with the consolidation of the non-operating current accounts of all parts of the economy, whether households, government departments or business enterprises. It is of course true that governments undertake certain activities on a commercial basis and in this case we shall wish to set up an operating account for them which will appear consolidated with the operating accounts of private enterprise; but on the whole these operating activities, even nowadays, will form but a comparatively small part of the total of government transactions.

Finally, the form of economic activity adding to wealth is the focus of transactions of a capital nature and as presented in the example I have given earlier is nothing more than the consolidation of the accounts of all parts of the economy which are devoted to capital transactions. Such an account, which is frequently referred to by economists as a capital account, is not normally provided explicitly in business accounting though it has been suggested that if provided it might go under the name 'resting account', since it is the account in which transactions, the effect of which is expected to last beyond the period of the account, rest until they are finally written off out of current incomings. In fact, however, as already mentioned, this account does nothing more than provide a link between the opening and closing balance sheet, and therefore the transactions which it contains are reflected in changes in the balance-sheet position.

We thus see that an accounting structure, consisting of operating accounts, non-operating accounts and changes in balance-sheet position, is isomorphic with a classification of economic activity into the three forms: production, consumption and adding to wealth. Furthermore, we have seen that although this accounting structure is normally only fully developed in the case of enterprises it nevertheless applies equally to all other entities in the economic system, and that it is only by consolidating each type of account over all entities that we can obtain the picture of transactions given in my earlier example.

XXI. STATISTICAL DESIGN IN SOCIAL ACCOUNTING

I mentioned earlier the desirability of introducing statistical design, as far as possible, into the procedure for collecting economic information in order to obtain the information in the most efficient way, to avoid bias and incompleteness, and to enable a measure of the reliability of the resulting estimates to be made. The field of social accounting is one in which a method of obtaining information which possesses these advantages is particularly desirable since here we are dealing with a system of empirical constructs which are related to one another. Moreover, measures of many of the component elements can only be made with considerable difficulty and uncertainty from information which already exists.

In attempting to demonstrate the isomorphism between the three types of account in a basic accounting structure and the three fundamental forms of economic activity I hope to have shown that it is possible in principle to collect the information required for social accounting investigations on an accounting basis. It is possible to draw up an accounting system which will reflect the kind of distinction in which we are interested as economists and it would be possible to use this system, appropriately modified and elaborated, for different parts of the economy as a basis on which to collect social accounting information. If this be granted then the difficulties we have to face are of a practical nature and the more important of them may be described as follows.

Having set up an accounting structure which makes use of the definitions and distinctions best suited for economic analysis, we have to see that this information can be obtained in practice from available records. This problem arises in a sense whatever method of collecting information is adopted, but it has to be faced explicitly if we start with a definite demand for information of a particular kind rather than with an acceptance of primary data as they already exist.

As far as business enterprises are concerned it can be seen that the accounting structure desired is not very different from the accounting structure in actual use. On many points of detail accounting conventions are satisfactory from the standpoint of an economist, but there are two kinds of problem which deserve special mention. In the first place, from a social accounting point of view, it is desirable as far as possible to obtain a 'to whom from whom' classification of transactions within each of the main headings in the accounts. For example, it is necessary to know as far as possible how much of the total sales proceeds of an enterprise has been contributed by sales to each of the different sectors of the economy. In the second place questions arise over the basis of valuation of fixed assets and inventories in which the current accounting conventions do not lead to the information which the economist would like to have, although he would be very much better off with a complete statement embodying existing accounting conventions than he is at the present time when in the case of inventories at any rate very little information of any kind is available. These and a number of similar questions call for a comparison of the information sought by the economist and the information normally available in accounting records, with the object of seeing how far by an appropriate change in the way in which questions are asked, information needed by the economist can be obtained from business records as they are kept at present, and how far some change in existing book-keeping methods is required. This aspect of the matter is at present under investigation by Bray.*

In the case of public authorities similar problems arise and certain additional ones besides. As far as local authorities are concerned considerable headway has been made in this country by the application of sampling methods to local authority accounts, the basis of collection being an accounting questionnaire designed to provide much of the information wanted for social accounting purposes. This approach has been developed by J. E. G. Utting of the National Institute of Economic and Social Research and a brief indication of the kind of information which he has been able to collect has now been published.†

In the case of the central government the position is more difficult. Local authorities in this country make a distinction between current and capital accounts and also keep their accounts on an income and expenditure basis. The central government on the other hand does not make the distinction between current and capital accounts, at least not in any economically meaningful way, and the accounts themselves are kept on a cash basis. By means of numerous reclassifications and adjustments the compilers of the national income White Paper have contrived to present the accounts of the central government in a form which is as close to what is required for social accounting purposes as possible. This task would, however, be immensely eased and the resulting estimates would be accordingly increased in reliability if the accounting machine of the central government could in its definitions and form of presentation go further than it does at present to provide the data needed for

* See *Social Accounts and the Business Enterprise Sector of the National Economy* (1949), by F. Sewell Bray. This study is no. 2 in the Monograph Series of the Department of Applied Economics, Cambridge.

† See 'Social Accounting: Some First Results of the Enquiry', in *Local Government Finance* (January 1949), pp. 9–12, and 'The Social Accounting Inquiry for 1947–48', ibid. (December 1949), pp. 289–90. The full results of this investigation will be published in due course in the series of *Occasional Papers* issued by the National Institute.

social accounting purposes. Suggestions of various ways in which this might be done have been made recently by F. S. Bray and myself* and by J. R. Hicks.† The principal difficulties as they stand at the moment relate first to classification and presentation, second to the cash basis of the accounts, and third to the lack of any meaningful distinction between current and capital transactions. The first of these difficulties could almost wholly be overcome without departing from the basic principles on which the central government accounts are at present prepared, and considerable progress in dealing with the third problem could also be made by means of an improved form of classification of the items as they are presented at the present time.

In the case of individual households the difficulty is of course that very little exact information is available so that there is a large field for experimentation in the best method of collecting information from this source. One approach would be to induce a sample of households to keep records for a period on the desired lines. An important difficulty here would be that the households which could be induced to do this might not be typical of households in general. Another line of approach is to visit households at the end of an accounting period and ask for estimates of accounting items in the period just passed. The difficulty here is to obtain reliable estimates since much of what took place will not have been recorded and will no longer be fresh in the mind of the respondent. An attempt may be made to improve the position by requiring that the accounting identities be satisfied by the information provided, but the difficulty here is that some of the information which may be only vaguely present in the mind of the respondent will be distorted, consciously or subconsciously, to meet the requirements of balance. Another approach therefore would be to visit two separate samples of households and ask one sample for data on incomings and the other for data on outgoings. It would be of great interest to know more about the reliability and representativeness of the information obtainable by these different methods of approach.

Throughout this discussion of statistical design I have emphasized the necessity of a sampling approach,‡ since from a practical point of view it is quite unthinkable that much of the information needed could be collected on the basis of complete returns from all entities. In sampling for economic information account must be taken of the characteristics of the population sampled and in particular of the extreme skewness of the size distribution of, for example, enterprises, local authorities or households. This suggests the desirability of some measure of stratification by size with different sampling ratios in each stratum,

* See 'The Presentation of the Central Government Accounts', in *Accounting Research*, vol. I, no. 1 (November 1948), pp. 1–12.
† See *The Problem of Budgetary Reform* (1948).
‡ See 'The Use of Sampling Methods in National Income Statistics and Social Accounting', by R. Stone, J. E. G. Utting and J. Durbin; cf. footnote * on p. 11 above.

or alternatively a method of selection of the sample from the population with probability of selection proportional to size. These methods entail some information on the size of the different elements in the population and call for discussion of the concept of size for sampling purposes. The concept of size from this point of view has been studied by J. Durbin in an unpublished paper read before the European meeting of the Econometric Society, 1948, dealing with sampling methods appropriate to business enterprises. There he showed that in fact in a sample of American companies in the iron and steel and engineering industries there was a high correlation between the different main profit and loss account and balance-sheet items, so that for example total sales proceeds or total assets as shown in the balance sheet would be an appropriate measure of size in sampling for other items in the accounts. In the same way Utting's investigation into local authorities indicates a similar high correlation between the different main accounting items, so that for example rates received could be taken as a measure of size, not only in sampling for rate account items, but also in sampling for items in the trading accounts of local authorities. This empirical fact that a large part of the variability of accounting entries for given types of entity such as enterprises, local authorities, etc., is absorbed by one principal component, is obviously a matter of considerable importance from a sampling point of view and can be used to improve the efficiency of sampling methods. Once the information has been obtained a further improvement may be expected from an adjustment of the entries designed to make them consistent. We have already seen that a system of n connected accounts contains $(n-1)$ constraints. If, however, each transaction or block of transactions can be measured twice, e.g. if an estimate of wages can be made independently from the accounts of employers and of employees, then clearly a large number of further constraints are available which can be used to reduce the error in the estimates.

Although the intensive study of the problem of sampling design in the collection of economic and social data is a comparatively recent one, nevertheless it may be hoped that a number of the purely statistical problems can be anticipated and solved with the aid of the experience that we already have. As I suggested earlier, it seems probable that the most intractable problems lie in the field of obtaining an accurate response from a representative fraction of the population sampled. There can be little doubt that this aspect of the problem will receive much attention in the next few years.

XXII. MARKET DEMAND FROM THE VIEWPOINT OF ECONOMIC THEORY

In this and the following sections I shall illustrate the steps involved in testing hypotheses and estimating parameters, and this I propose to do by taking the example of the analysis of market demand. Here we have essentially two questions: first, Is the ordinary demand theory, or some suitable modification of it, capable of explaining observed variations in the demand for different commodities?; second, if so, What are the most acceptable estimates of the demand parameters, particularly the income and price elasticities, and what is the reliability of these estimates? An investigation of these problems involves first, an examination of the economic and social factors affecting demand, and second, an examination of the statistical problems of testing the significance of the relationship finally arrived at, and of estimating the parameters in this relationship.

It is usual to base the analysis of market demand on a study of individual demand. From this point of view it is convenient to assume that in a market of N consumers, who may in general have different incomes, but face the same set of prices, an indifference map for each consumer is well defined in accordance with the postulates of individual demand theory,* incomes and prices being non-negative. In each individual case the quantity demanded is an exact function of the individual's income and all the prices, and so the amount demanded by the whole market, obtained simply by summing the amount demanded by each individual, depends on all the incomes and all the prices. In other words,

$$q_{in} = f_{in}(\mu_n, p_1, ..., p_I) \tag{65}$$

and
$$q_i = \sum_{n=i}^{N} q_{in} \qquad \begin{aligned} i &= 1, 2, ..., I, \\ n &= 1, 2, ..., N, \end{aligned} \tag{66}$$

where q_i is the amount demanded of commodity i by the market composed of N individuals.

From the assumptions made about the individual demand relationships it follows that the market relations satisfy two conditions. The first is usually termed the balance relationship and may be stated in the form

$$\sum_i \sum_n p_i q_{in} = \sum_n \mu_n, \tag{67}$$

where p_i is the price of the ith commodity and μ_n is the income of the nth individual. The second type of relationship is one of proportionality, which states that if each income and each price is multiplied by a factor k the amount demanded is unchanged, or, in symbols,

$$q_i = f_i(\mu_1, ..., \mu_N, p_1, ..., p_I) = f_i(k\mu_1, ..., k\mu_N, kp_1, ..., kp_I). \tag{68}$$

Further the following theorems hold with respect to market demand.

First, the elasticity of market demand with respect to any price is a weighted average of the corresponding individual elasticities, the weights being the quantities demanded by the individual consumers. This may

---

* For a precise description of what this condition entails, see 'A Synthesis of Pure Demand Analysis', by H. O. A. Wold, in *Skandinavisk Aktuarietidskrift* (1943), pp. 85–118, 222–63, and (1944), pp. 69–120.

be stated in the following form:

$$\frac{\partial \sum_n q_{in} \; p_j}{\partial p_j \; \sum_n q_{in}} = \sum_n \frac{\left\{\frac{\partial q_{in}}{\partial p_j}\frac{p_j}{q_{in}} q_{in}\right\}}{\sum_n q_{in}}. \tag{69}$$

Second, assuming that all incomes vary in the same proportion, the income elasticity of market demand of any commodity is a weighted average of the individual elasticities, the weights being the quantities demanded by the individual consumers. In symbols we may write

$$\frac{\Delta \sum_n q_{in} \sum_n \mu_n}{\Delta \sum_n \mu_n \sum_n q_{in}} = \frac{\sum_n \left\{\frac{\partial q_{in}}{\partial \mu_n}\frac{\mu_n}{q_{in}} q_{in}\right\}}{\sum_n q_{in}}, \tag{70}$$

where Δ denotes an infinitesimal increment in total quantity when the μ's are changing in proportion.

Third, again assuming that all incomes vary in the same proportion, the income elasticity of market demand for any commodity equals minus the sum of the price and cross elasticities of the same demand. This may be written in symbols:

$$\frac{\Delta \sum_n q_{in} \sum_n \mu_n}{\Delta \sum_n \mu_n \sum_n q_{in}} = -\sum_j \left\{\frac{\partial \sum_n q_{in}}{\partial p_j}\frac{p_j}{\sum_n q_{in}}\right\}. \tag{71}$$

Fourth, taking expenditures as weights, the weighted average of the market's income elasticities for all commodities is unity; or, in symbols,

$$\frac{\sum_i \left\{\frac{\Delta \sum_n q_{in} \sum_n \mu_n}{\Delta \sum_n \mu_n \sum_n q_{in}} \sum_n q_{in}p_i\right\}}{\sum_i \sum_n q_{in}p_i} = 1. \tag{72}$$

Fifth, again taking expenditures as weights, the negative of the weighted average of the market's demand elasticities formed with respect to the price of a given commodity equals the proportion of total income spent on this commodity; or, in symbols,

$$\frac{\sum_i \left\{\frac{\partial \sum_n q_{in}}{\partial p_j}\frac{p_j}{\sum_n q_{in}} \sum_n q_{in}p_i\right\}}{\sum_i \sum_n q_{in}p_i} = -\frac{\sum_n q_{jn}p_j}{\sum_n \mu_n}, \tag{73}$$

in which the elasticities are referred to the jth commodity.

The pure theory of market demand makes the demand for any given commodity depend on the incomes of all the individuals and the prices of all the commodities. Stated in this form the theory is quite unmanageable from the practical point of view, since the demand for each commodity is made to depend on millions of incomes and at least thousands of prices. Some means must be found of reducing this enormous number of determining variables in each equation.

So far as incomes are concerned it is usual in practice to make the same assumption as is made in several of the above theorems, that all the incomes in the market vary in the same proportion, so that we can include as a determining variable simply the total income of all the individuals. It is known, however, that all incomes do not vary proportionately, and it would be desirable to take into account higher moments of the income distribution. Unfortunately, this is rarely possible, since satisfactory information is not as a rule available about even the dispersion of the income distribution, which would be the most obvious determining variable to introduce in addition to the total or average income. As a consequence care is needed in interpreting the apparent income elasticities derived from observation, although I shall refer to them as income elasticities in what follows.

As regards prices, the usual simplification is to introduce the price of the commodity and an index of all other prices, or at most to include as separate determining variables the prices of important substitutes for or complements to the commodity being studied. The approximate nature of this line of approach must be fully realized, since strictly speaking it is only justifiable to combine the prices of different commodities if those prices have all moved in the same proportion. In practice, this is almost certain not to have happened, although in many cases there will be a considerable correlation between the movements of the different prices combined. If it could be done, it would be a considerable improvement to introduce not individual prices at all but the first few principal components of the price complex, so as to make sure of representing fully the diverse components of the movement of prices. The analysis could be carried out in terms of these components and then if desired translated back into terms of at least the more important individual prices.

XXIII. OTHER INFLUENCES TO BE TAKEN INTO ACCOUNT

In the theory of individual demand it is assumed that each individual has a well-defined indifference map, different perhaps from that of every other individual, but unchanged over the period of analysis. In practice, however, it is to be expected that in the case of some commodities at any rate the preferences of individual consumers will change, with the consequence that pure economic theory will not provide us with a complete set of determining variables in the practical case. Accordingly, some attempt must be made to take account of changes in preferences if there is any reason to suppose that these have been important over the period for which the analyses are to be made. The usual means of doing this is to introduce time as a variable. The justification for this procedure is that generally speaking tastes will change only slowly and therefore a slowly moving residual trend will absorb variations in the amount demanded by the market due to changes in taste. It must be recognized, however, that this is a very crude device which ought to be replaced by an investigation of changes in preferences over time. For example, in the case of tobacco consumption in the United Kingdom, the last two generations have seen a very large change in the proportion of women smokers, so that a considerable amount of the upward trend in tobacco consumption could be accounted for if information were available for each year of the actual numbers of men and women who were smokers. Again, in relation to the economic factors, there seems to have been a considerable rise in tobacco consumption between 1914 and 1918, which may perhaps be attributed to a change in habits induced by the war. If this hypothesis be accepted an attempt to measure its influence can be made by introducing a variable which takes the value of 0 before 1914 and 1 after 1918. In this way the periods before and after World War I are brought roughly on to the same basis of preference.

In addition to these general changes in tastes, it is clear that demand is affected by a number of other factors which are not explicitly recognized in pure theory. An example of this is advertising and the practice which has been important in some trades at certain times of attracting custom by giving away gifts with purchases. Again preferences may be temporarily disturbed by the sheer novelty of some new technical development, as seems to have been the case with cinema attendance on the introduction of sound films at the end of the 1920's. In this case there appears to have been a sharp rise in attendances which is not capable of explanation in purely economic terms, and which died away shortly after the introduction of the novelty. From a practical point of view attention must be given to all factors of this kind with the object of introducing some variable into the analysis which will stand for the variation in the factors involved. One means of making a rough allowance for such a factor is to introduce a variable taking the values 0, 1, 0, the value 1 being taken in the years in which the particular influence was supposed to be operative. If in fact the influence was operative only in one year, then this proposal is equivalent to a proposal to omit the year in question altogether. The justification for such an omission is that we can distinguish a specific influence which does not enter into our hypothesis and which we are not bound to consider because its influence is confined to a single year.

XXIV. THE FORMULATION OF MARKET DEMAND RELATIONSHIPS

The determining variables which will be introduced into the following analysis are aggregate income in real or money terms, the price of the commodity in question and certain other price series or index numbers, time, and in certain cases special variables such as the strength of beer or a discontinuity factor of the type just described. For the sake of simplicity a form of equation will be chosen which involves the assumption that all elasticities are constants and that the residual trend reflects a constant proportionate rate of change per annum. Neglecting specific variables and combining all other prices in one index number, the resulting demand equation has the form

$$q = aR^b p^c \pi^d e^{rt+u},\qquad(74)$$

or
$$\log_e q = \log_e a + b\log_e R + c\log_e p + d\log_e \pi + rt + u,\qquad(75)$$

where q = the quantity demanded by a community of some commodity,

   R = the aggregate real income of the community,

   p = the price of the commodity,

   π = an index of the prices of all other commodities,

   t = time,

   u = a residual, representing the variation in q not accounted for by the preceding influences.

The null hypothesis here is that any correlation between q on the one hand and R, p, π and t on the other may be ascribed to chance. This hypothesis may be tested by computing the multiple correlation coefficient between the dependent and the determining variables and will be rejected if this coefficient is significantly different from zero. The rejection of the null hypothesis means that given the size of the sample the correlation between the dependent and the determining variables is greater than could be expected as a result of sampling fluctuations between two sets of series which are in truth unrelated. What is to be expected depends on the level of significance chosen and this is determined by our willingness to be wrong from time to time as the price of reaching any conclusions at all. It is usual to choose the 5 per cent level of significance; this means that in the long run we are prepared to be wrong (that is, claim relationships on the basis of sample information where we ought not to do so) in 5 per cent of the cases. If we were to lower our standards we could make more positive statements but they would turn out more frequently to be wrong. If we were to raise our standards we should make fewer mistakes but also fewer statements. We have to choose therefore between making mistakes and failing to draw conclusions, between reckless assertion and silence.

If the null hypothesis is defeated we may say that the evidence points to a relationship between q on the one hand and R, p, π and t on the other, which we should see confirmed if we had more information available. We may then proceed to calculate the parameters a, b, c, d and r which reflect respectively a scale constant, the income elasticity of demand (strictly, on the assumption that all incomes vary in proportion), the own-price substitution elasticity, the substitution elasticity with respect to the average of other prices and the proportionate rate of change per annum of the residual trend. We may test the significance of these parameters by calculating their standard errors and applying the t-test. If we find that one of them, say b, is not significantly different from zero this does not of course mean that its value is zero—clearly the best estimate of its value is the one we have made. It means that any hypothesis which entails that this parameter is zero is not rejected by the observations.

Defining money income $\sum_n \mu_n \equiv M \equiv PR$, where $P = \prod_i p^{w_i}$ and $w_i = \sum_n p_i q_{in} / M$ so that $\sum_i w_i = 1$, we see that (74) is exactly equivalent to

$$q = a' M^b p^{(c-bw)} \pi^{[d-b(1-w)]} e^{rt+u}, \tag{76}$$

where the price elasticities, $(c - bw)$ and $[d - b(1 - w)]$, have their usual meanings being compounded of the price-substitution effects, c and d respectively, and the income-effects, bw and $b(1 - w)$ respectively. In practice we may expect that the relationship between the elasticities of a formulation involving real income and a formulation involving money income will not be exactly as shown in (74) and (76) since in practice the measures of the general level of prices, P, and the level of all other prices, π, will not be weighted geometric means.

Let us look at these formulations from the point of view of the balance relationship and the proportionality relationship. As regards the balance relationship it is clearly not possible for all commodities to be expressed by equations which are linear in the logarithms of incomes, prices and quantities since this would involve inconsistency. This can be seen if from the balance equation we express the amount demanded of one commodity, say q_i, in terms of the other quantities, prices and income, thus obtaining

$$q_i = (M - \sum_{j \neq i} p_j q_j) p_i^{-1}, \tag{77}$$

and then substitute for each q_i an expression of the form

$$\alpha M^\beta \prod_{i=1}^{I} p_i^{\gamma_i},$$

for the expression thus obtained for q_i is not of the form just given. Thus the simple logarithmic formulation would not be satisfactory if we wanted a complete set of equations all of the same form to express the whole pattern of demand. It may, however, be satisfactory as a convenient approximation to any case taken separately.

The proportionality condition requires that in (76) the sum

$$b + (c - bw) + [d - b(1 - w)] = 0,$$

or

$$c + d = 0, \tag{78}$$

i.e. that the sum of the price-substitution elasticities is zero. We may test the hypothesis that this condition is not satisfied in any case by computing the standard error of this sum of the price-substitution elasticities and comparing the standard error with the sum itself. Alternatively we may assume that the proportionality condition is satisfied, in which case a suitable formulation involving real income would be

$$q = \alpha R^\beta (p/\pi)^\gamma e^{rt+u}, \tag{79}$$

while one involving money income would be

$$q = \alpha' (M/p)^{\beta'} (M/\pi)^{\gamma'} e^{rt+u}. \tag{80}$$

XXV. STATISTICAL PROBLEMS

If one of the formulations of the preceding section be accepted the next step is to compute the multiple correlation coefficient and estimate the parameters connecting the variables. This involves the use of multi-variate regression techniques and under ideal conditions could be accomplished by applying the method of least squares. For example if we accepted the formulation (74) we might first transform q, R, p and π into their logarithms and then in (75) estimate $\log a$, b, c, d and r so as to minimize the sum of the squares of the u's.

The application of this method to the data as they stand requires that certain conditions be fulfilled. First, the discrepancy or residual must be distributed independently in different years with mean zero and con-stant variance and this distribution must strictly speaking be normal if the usual tests of significance are to be applied. Second, the determining variables must be observed without error, the discrepancy being attribut-able either to errors in the dependent variable or to the influence of factors which are omitted. Finally, the sampling model implies that the determining variables may be regarded as fixed in repeated samples while the dependent variable is free to vary as a consequence of the influences just mentioned. If these assumptions do not hold in practice various difficulties arise which may be briefly mentioned.

(1) *The Serial Correlation Problem*

This problem arises if the first assumption is not fulfilled, that is if the residuals show some degree of interrelation over time. Consideration was given to this source of difficulty by Aitken[*] and more recently the problem has been studied with specific reference to economic time series by Champernowne[†] and by Cochrane and Orcutt.[‡] We may approach the problem by considering the autoregressive properties of the dis-crepancy, u, in (75). If u may be regarded as a random normal deviate then no problem arises. But in practice we usually find some association between neighbouring values of u so that u can be approximated by an

[*] See 'On Least Squares and Linear Combinations of Observations', by A. C. Aitken, in *Proceedings of the Royal Society of Edinburgh*, vol. LV (1934–35), pp. 42–8.

[†] See 'Sampling Theory Applied to Autoregressive Sequences', by D. G. Champer-nowne, in *Journal of the Royal Statistical Society* (Series B), vol. X, no. 2 (1948), pp. 204–31.

[‡] See 'Application of Least Squares Regression to Relationships containing Auto-correlated Error Terms', by D. Cochrane and G. H. Orcutt, in *Journal of the American Statistical Association*, vol. XLIV, no. 245 (March 1949), pp. 32–61.

autoregressive equation. Suppose that

$$u = E^{-1}u + \epsilon, \tag{81}$$

where ϵ is a random deviate. If we apply the transformation $(1 - E^{-1}) = \Delta'$ say, to all the variables in (75), i.e. if we take first differences instead of the original series, then evidently the residual in the transformed equation will be ϵ and since the first condition is now satisfied the standard methods can be applied. In order to make an appropriate transformation we must have a means of testing any series of residuals for serial dependence. This may be done approximately by computing von Neumann's ratio, the ratio of the mean square successive difference to the variance, for the series of residuals. Denoting this ratio by v and the number of sets of observations by N we define

$$v = \frac{N}{(N-1)} \frac{\Sigma(\Delta'u)^2}{\Sigma(u-\bar{u})^2}, \tag{82}$$

where $\bar{u}$ is the mean value of the residual over the period of observation. It has been shown that for a random series the expected value of v is given by

$$E(v) = \frac{2N}{(N-1)}, \tag{83}$$

and the variance $V(v)$ is given by

$$V(v) = \frac{4N^2(N-2)}{(N-1)^3(N+1)}. \tag{84}$$

Champernowne, in the paper referred to, has considered the problem of estimating the parameters in a generalized version of (81) simultaneously with the estimation of the parameters in (75). Cochrane and Orcutt on the other hand have adopted a more empirical approach and shown that in a large number of actual cases the simple first difference transformation, Δ', will lead to residuals that are appropriately distributed around a value approximating the expected value in (83). The analyses given in the next section are in accord with these findings. In the analyses of American data in Section xxvii, however, acceptable values of v are obtained without transformation.

(2) *The Confluence Problem*

Little need be said about this problem which has been considered exhaustively by Frisch* and Koopmans† and applied to demand analysis in an earlier paper of my own.‡ It is sufficient to say that if the second assumption is not fulfilled, that is if it cannot be assumed that the determining variables are measured without error, then it is particularly

* See *Confluence Analysis by Means of Complete Regression Systems*, by R. Frisch (1934).
† See *Linear Regression Analysis of Economic Time Series*, by T. Koopmans (1937).
‡ See 'The Analysis of Market Demand', by R. Stone, in *Journal of the Royal Statistical Society*, vol. cviii, pts. iii and iv (1945), pp. 1–98.

important that there should be one and only one relationship connecting the set of variables, not only in the population but also in the sample. For example if by chance, over a twenty-year period, one variable in the analysis happens to have moved steadily upwards then it will not be possible with the information available to apportion the variation of the dependent variable between this variable and time. Of course we may leave time out of the analysis, but we then run the risk of attributing to the steadily moving variable variation in the dependent variable which is properly attributable to the influences which time has been introduced to represent. Furthermore, if two variables, neither of which is time, move together we may not have this possibility of leaving one of them out while retaining a formulation of the demand relationship which can be interpreted. It will be seen that this is essentially the identification problem over again except that lack of identifiability may not be apparent from the formal study of a system of relationships since it may arise only as a sampling phenomenon. Frisch's method of bunch-maps is intended to indicate the presence of unexpected relationships and generally to help in the decision of whether the inclusion of a given variable in a given analysis is helpful, superfluous or detrimental.

(3) *The Problem of Errors in Variables*

If the second assumption is not fulfilled it is reasonable to expect that bias will be introduced into the estimates of the parameters. Let us write each variable in the form $x_i \equiv x_i' + x_i''$, where the observed variable x_i is made up of a systematic part or true value x_i' and an error term x_i''. In a two variable problem involving X_1 and X_2 we should like to take as our estimator of the regression of X_1 on X_2 the ratio $\Sigma x_1' x_2' / \Sigma x_2'^2$. In fact, however, if we work with the observed variables, we shall be forced, if we apply the standard methods, to take an estimator of the form

$$\frac{\Sigma(x_1'+x_1'')(x_2'+x_2'')}{\Sigma(x_2'+x_2'')^2} = \frac{\Sigma x_1' x_2' + \Sigma x_1' x_2'' + \Sigma x_1'' x_2' + \Sigma x_1'' x_2''}{\Sigma x_2'^2 + 2\Sigma x_2' x_2'' + \Sigma x_2''^2}. \tag{85}$$

If we assume, as is frequently done, that the error components of any two variables are uncorrelated and that the same is true of the error component of any variable and the systematic part of the same or any other variable, i.e.

$$\Sigma x_i' x_i'' = \Sigma x_i' x_j'' = \Sigma x_i'' x_j'' = 0, \tag{86}$$

then the right-hand side of (85) reduces to

$$\frac{\Sigma x_1' x_2'}{\Sigma x_2'^2 + \Sigma x_2''^2},$$

which is biased downwards since the second term in the denominator, being a sum of squares, is necessarily positive.

In the case in which no information is available about the variance-covariance matrix of the error components, methods of overcoming this bias have been proposed by Reiersøl* and Geary.† If such information is available or can be estimated from the data, then the more refined methods proposed by Tintner‡ can be employed.

(4) The Problem of Errors in Equations

If the equation studied is subject to error and one of a set of simultaneous equations then in general the third assumption cannot be fulfilled. The form of the maximum likelihood solution in such a case can be obtained, but the resulting equations can only be solved by approximate means and are very difficult to handle. The use of the method of least squares in these circumstances can be justified theoretically in two cases. First, if the model of which the equation studied forms a part is a sequence-model or *recursive* in the sense of Bentzel and Wold.§ Second, if the system of equations containing the equation studied is first transformed to the reduced form, i.e. if each endogenous variable is expressed in terms of predetermined variables which comprise past values of these variables and exogenous variables which act on but are not acted on by the endogenous variables of the model. I do not propose to go further into these problems here and shall only refer to the works of Haavelmo,‖ Mann and Wald,¶ Koopmans** and Girshick.†† The

* See 'Confluence Analysis by Means of Lag Moments and Other Methods of Confluence Analysis', in *Econometrica*, vol. IX, no. 1 (January 1941), pp. 1–24; 'Confluence Analysis by Means of Instrumental Sets of Variables', in *Arkiv för Matematik, Astronomi och Fysik*, Band 32A, no. 4 (1945).

† See 'Inherent Relations between Random Variables', in *Proceedings of the Royal Irish Academy*, vol. XLVII, section A, no. 6 (1942), pp. 63–76; 'Relations between Statistics: the General and Sampling Problem when the Samples are Large', ibid. vol. XLIX, section A, no. 10 (1943), pp. 177–96; 'Determination of Unbiased Linear Relations between the Systematic Parts of Variables with Errors of Observation', in *Econometrica*, vol. XVII, no. 1 (January 1949), pp. 30–58.

‡ See 'An Application of the Variate Difference Method to Multiple Regression', in *Econometrica*, vol. XII, no. 2 (April 1944), pp. 97–113; 'A Note on Rank, Multicollinearity and Multiple Regression', in *Annals of Mathematical Statistics*, vol. XVI, no. 3 (September 1945), pp. 304–8; 'Multiple Regression for Systems of Equations', in *Econometrica*, vol. XIV, no. 1 (January 1946), pp. 5–36; 'Some Applications of Multivariate Analysis to Economic Data', in *Journal of the American Statistical Association*, vol. XLI (December 1946), pp. 472–500.

§ See 'On Statistical Demand Analysis from the Viewpoint of Simultaneous Equations', in *Skandinavisk Aktuarietidskrift*, vol. XXIX, nos. 1 and 2 (1946), pp. 95–114.

‖ See 'The Statistical Implications of a System of Simultaneous Equations', in *Econometrica*, vol. XI, no. 1 (January 1943), pp. 1–12.

¶ See 'On the Statistical Treatment of Linear Stochastic Difference Equations', in *Econometrica*, vol. XI, nos. 3 and 4 (July–October 1943), pp. 173–220.

** See 'Statistical Estimation of Simultaneous Economic Relations', in *Journal of the American Statistical Association*, vol. XL, no. 232, pt. 1 (December 1945), pp. 448–66; *Statistical Methods of Measuring Economic Relationships* (notes by C. Christ on a course of lectures by T. Koopmans, circulated in mimeographed form by the Cowles Commission).

†† See 'Statistical Analysis of the Demand for Food: Examples of Simultaneous Estimation of Structural Equations', by M. A. Girshick and T. Haavelmo, in *Econometrica*, vol. XV, no. 2 (April 1947), pp. 79–110.

results obtained by these writers rest essentially on large-sample theory and it has been shown by Orcutt and Cochrane* that in small samples the reduced form method may give seriously misleading results.

XXVI. DEMAND ANALYSES FOR THE UNITED KINGDOM

In Table 3 there are shown the results of thirteen demand analyses for the United Kingdom covering the period 1920–38. I do not propose to describe the methods and data used in detail since much is available in two earlier articles† and the data used will be fully described in a forthcoming book.‡ Analyses on a similar basis over the much longer period 1870–1938 have been given recently for a number of commodities by Prest.§ All that need be said here is that the estimates of the parameters and their standard errors are based not on the original data but on the first differences of these and that in all cases the method of bunchmaps was applied and as a consequence certain possible determining variables were rejected. The form of the equation adopted was chosen from among those set out in Section XXIV, usually either (74) or (79), modified where necessary to exclude certain variables or to include special variables. In the case of butter and margarine the income elasticity of demand was estimated from budget data and (qR^{-b}) was taken as the dependent variable. In the case of butter, margarine and imported potatoes a third price variable was introduced representing respectively the price of margarine, of butter and of home-produced potatoes. In the cases of margarine, beer and tobacco a special variable was introduced. In the analysis of margarine an allowance was made for a break in conditions in 1922–3 to reflect the change believed to have occurred in the availability of fats between the years following World War I and the middle 1920's. The strength of the beer was introduced into the beer analysis and the preceding year's relative prices were introduced into the analysis of tobacco.

The interpretation of the parameters in the first-difference form can be seen by applying the first-difference transformation to (75). The first term on the right-hand side, being a constant, will disappear on multiplication by Δ'. The term in t on the other hand will become a constant since $\Delta'rt = r$. It is this constant in each case that has been taken as

* See 'A Sampling Study of the Merits of Autoregressive and Reduced Form Transformations in Regression Analysis', in *Journal of the American Statistical Association*, vol. XLIV, no. 247 (September 1949), pp. 356–72.

† See 'The Analysis of Market Demand', loc. cit. (1945), and 'The Analysis of Market Demand: an Outline of Methods and Results', in *Review of the International Statistical Institute*, vol. XVI, nos. 1–4 (1948), pp. 23–35.

‡ See *Consumers' Expenditure in the United Kingdom*, 1920–1938, vol. I, to be published in the forthcoming series of Studies in the National Income and Expenditure of the United Kingdom sponsored jointly by the National Institute of Economic and Social Research and the Department of Applied Economics.

§ See 'Some Experiments in Demand Analysis', by A. R. Prest, in *Review of Economics and Statistics*, vol. XXI, no. 1 (February 1949), pp. 33–49.

TABLE 3. SUMMARY OF DEMAND ANALYSES FOR THE UNITED KINGDOM BASED ON FIRST DIFFERENCES OF ANNUAL DATA OVER THE PERIOD 1920–38

Commodity	Income elasticity	Substitution elasticities			Other factors	Residual trend	$\bar{R}^2$	v
		Own price	Related price	All other prices				
Butter	0·46	−0·40±0·16	0·09±0·18	0·30±0·21	...	0·030±0·010	0·21	1·91
Cream	...	−0·89±0·41	...	0·75±0·69	...	0·060±0·022	0·17	2·85
Margarine	−0·43	0·42±0·22	0·89±0·26	1·31±0·28	0·26±0·80	0·005±0·015	0·57	2·31
Lard	−0·08±0·40	−0·60±0·10	...	0·60±0·10	...	−0·004±0·016	0·75	2·06
Home-produced potatoes	0·32±0·29	−0·57±0·07	...	0·43±0·26	...	−0·007±0·013	0·81	2·02
Imported potatoes	...	−1·27±0·24	1·71±0·25	−0·44±0·37	...	−0·006±0·049	0·83	2·34
Beer	...	−0·69±0·11	...	0·94±0·07	1·16±0·35	0·007±0·003	0·95	2·01
Spirits	0·60±0·14	−0·57±0·12	...	0·57±0·12	...	−0·033±0·006	0·77	2·63
Imported wine	0·98±0·33	−1·17±0·43	...	0·91±0·37	...	0·007±0·014	0·57	1·84
Tobacco	0·25±0·07	−0·27±0·06	...	0·27±0·06	−0·26±0·07	0·031±0·003	0·82	1·49
Soap	0·25±0·09	−0·24±0·12	...	0·24±0·12	...	0·018±0·004	0·28	1·97
Telegrams	0·16±0·20	−0·73±0·10	...	0·58±0·21	...	−0·014±0·007	0·93	1·65
Correspondence	0·21±0·15	−0·26±0·14	...	0·21±0·11	...	0·018±0·045	0·19	3·00

a measure of the rate of change of the residual trend. Since no attempt has been made in these analyses to correct consumption or income for the number of consumers, the residual trend will reflect the gradual increase in the number of consumers as well as any change there may have been in tastes, habits and the like.

The conclusions to be derived from these analyses, in so far as they are not immediately apparent from Table 3, may be summarized as follows.

(1) *Justification for First Difference Transformation*

There are eighteen sets of observations and with $N = 18$ the expected value and standard error of von Neumann's ratio for a random series is $2 \cdot 12 \pm 0 \cdot 46$. The equivalent statistics for the mean of thirteen series are $2 \cdot 12 \pm 0 \cdot 13$. The mean of the thirteen observed values is $2 \cdot 16$ and the difference $0 \cdot 04$ is clearly not significant. The variance calculated from (84) is $0 \cdot 211$ while the variance of the thirteen observed values is $0 \cdot 202$ and the ratio, $1 \cdot 04$, is also clearly not significant. On the other hand, if we had used the original series the expected value and standard error of von Neumann's ratio for the mean of thirteen series would have been $2 \cdot 11 \pm 0 \cdot 13$. The observed mean derived from the thirteen analyses is $1 \cdot 38$ and the difference $0 \cdot 73$ is some five times the standard error. We may conclude therefore that the values of the ratio obtained from analyses with first differences are consistent with the hypothesis that the residuals are random over time while those derived from analyses with the original series are not.

(2) *Evidence for Presence of Demand Relationships*

Having established that the residuals are approximately random we may test the significance of the postulated relationship, believed in each case to be the only one subsisting between the variables on the basis of bunch-map analysis, by testing whether or not the mean square ascribable to the regression equation is significantly greater than the mean square of deviations from the regression. This is equivalent to testing the significance of the multiple correlation coefficient R. Of the thirteen cases, nine are significant at the 1 per cent level. The remaining four, those for butter, cream, soap and correspondence, are not significant at the 5 per cent level though in each of these cases $R > 0 \cdot 5$.

(3) *The Individual Regression Coefficients and Their Significance*

An examination of Table 3 indicates that in the great majority of cases the signs of the elasticities are in accordance with theoretical expectations.

(a) *Income elasticities.* Those for butter and margarine are derived from budget studies.* In the case of cream, imported potatoes and beer

* See *Food, Health and Income* (2nd edit. 1937), by J. B. Orr, appendix VI, table III. Regressions of the logarithms of butter and of margarine expenditure per head on the logarithms of total food expenditure were calculated and multiplied by an assumed income elasticity of food expenditure of $0 \cdot 5$.

the influence of income was rejected by the bunch-map analysis. Of the remaining eight cases only four, spirits, imported wine, tobacco and soap, showed income elasticities significantly different from zero. The difficulty in interpreting these coefficients on account of the assumption of proportional movements in each individual income, referred to in Section XXII, must be kept in mind.

(b) *Own-price substitution elasticities.* As expected on theoretical grounds all these elasticities are negative with one exception. The exceptional case, margarine, cannot be analysed properly with the simple approach adopted here because of the close relationship over the period between butter and margarine prices which in theory should have elasticities with opposite signs. In ten cases these elasticities are significant, the exceptional cases being margarine, soap and correspondence.

(c) *Related-price substitution elasticities.* As can be seen from Table 3 the price of a related commodity is introduced in only three cases and in each case, the related commodity being a substitute, the elasticity is, as expected, positive. In two cases, where the price of butter is introduced into the analysis of margarine consumption and where the price of home-produced potatoes is introduced into the analysis of the consumption of imported potatoes, the elasticities are significant. It is hardly to be expected that in the third case in which the price of margarine is introduced into the analysis of butter consumption the substitution elasticity should be significant. For in theory the two elasticities of substitution, of butter with respect to margarine and of margarine with respect to butter, are equal. Denote these respectively by σ_{12} and σ_{21}. Since these are equal respectively to c_{12}/w_2 and c_{21}/w_1, where the two c's are substitution elasticities and the w's are the proportions of income devoted to the two commodities, it follows that

$$c_{12} = c_{21}w_2/w_1. \tag{87}$$

The ratio, w_2/w_1, of the expenditure on margarine to the expenditure on butter is approximately $0\cdot1$. Hence from the margarine analysis of Table 3 we should expect to find $c_{12} = 0\cdot09$ as we do. For this estimate to be significant its standard error would have to be $0\cdot04$ or less and, as can be seen from the table, this degree of accuracy is nowhere attainable with the available data.

(d) *All-other-price substitution elasticities.* In eleven cases this elasticity is positive in accordance with theoretical expectations. In the two exceptional cases, margarine and imported potatoes, there is a strong positive elasticity with respect to the price of a related commodity. This elasticity is significant in only seven cases: margarine, lard, beer, spirits, imported wine, tobacco and telegrams.

(e) *Other factors.* The nature of these has already been described. In each case the coefficient is significant.

(f) *Residual trends.* Significant positive residual trends are shown in six cases: butter, cream, beer, tobacco, soap and correspondence. A significant negative residual trend is shown in the case of spirits.

(4) *How far is the Proportionality Condition Satisfied?*

Some light can be thrown on this question by comparing the sum of the substitution elasticities with the standard error of this sum in the six cases in which these elasticities were determined without restriction. In five cases, namely, cream, home-produced potatoes, imported wine, telegrams and correspondence, the sum of the price-substitution elasticities was not significantly different from zero. In one case, beer, the difference was significant.*

XXVII. DEMAND ANALYSES FOR THE UNITED STATES OF AMERICA

For the United States of America over the years 1929–41 I have carried out demand analyses on a more extended plan with the aid of the series provided in the *Survey of Current Business*.† Table 4 (at end) sets out in nearly all cases a number of analyses using different combinations of determining variables. The reason for this is not that each analysis is believed to be of equal interest and reliability as an expression of the demand relationship, but simply that by studying a number of equations for each commodity we can trace the influence of adding (or leaving out) variables in making demand analyses. In view of the frequent use of the regression of the amount demanded on income alone or on income and a trend‡ it will be of particular interest to see how these combinations of variables work out in relation to other possible sets.

The conclusions to be drawn from this table may be summarized, in the order adopted in the last section, as follows.

(1) *The Use of Untransformed Data*

Most of the analyses shown here had been completed before the utility of using transformed series had been recognized. It was not thought worth while to recalculate the equations using first differences and so no justification can be given for the choice of untransformed variables. As will shortly be seen the residuals in the larger subsets at any rate show, on the average, values of von Neumann's ratio similar to those expected for random series of the same length. But this may be due to the 'bias towards randomness' discussed by Cochrane and Orcutt§ and does not ensure that the standard errors bear their usual

---

* But see the concluding paragraph of the next section on p. 80, below.

† For a statement of the sources used, see Section xxviii below.

‡ See 'Retail Sales and Consumer Income since VJ Day', by L. J. Paradiso, in *S.C.B.* (October 1946), pp. 10–17, and 'Retail Sales and Consumer Income', by C. Winston and Mabel A. Smith in *S.C.B.* (October 1948), pp. 12–19 and 23.

§ Op. cit. p. 45.

interpretation and can be accepted as measures of reliability in the ordinary sense. However, the failure to use an appropriate transformation will mean not so much that the estimates of the regression coefficients will be biased as that we may, by calculating standard errors, mislead ourselves as to the accuracy of these estimates. Thus the regression coefficients may be of interest in themselves and the findings of the last section suggest that the standard errors may not be altogether unreliable.

With so many analyses available it is possible to compare the means of the actual values of von Neumann's ratio for the residuals in different subsets of variables with those expected from a random series of the same length. For this purpose we may work with the groups (12), (125), (134), (1234), (1345) and (12345), where the numbers 1 to 5 stand respectively for the amount demanded, real income, the price of the commodity, the average price of all other consumers' goods and services and time. The first four of these variables are in every case in logarithmic form.* The numbers in other subsets are not very numerous and so can hardly be tested in this way. The results are shown in Table 5.

The mean values of v as calculated from the sets (12) and (134) differ from the expected value for a random series by many times their standard error, so we may conclude that on the present test these two subsets are quite unacceptable. The difference is also large in relation to the standard error in the case of (125) and even (1345) so we may perhaps reject these as well. This leaves only the sets (1234) and (12345) as acceptable on this test and these, of course, are the only ones which are really acceptable from the economic point of view.

In the case of the marginal set (1345) and the acceptable sets (1234) and (12345) it is of interest to see how far the dispersion of the ratios conforms with what is to be expected on the hypothesis that the series are random. Table 6 shows that the actual and expected dispersions are fairly similar and that their differences are small compared with the standard error of the expected values.

Thus in the present case we find, in contrast with our previous experience with British data, that if we are prepared to work with reasonably complete sets of variables and not with small subsets, we obtain on the average values of von Neumann's ratio which might have been obtained for random series.

(2) Evidence for Presence of Demand Relationships

Since the analyses have been conducted with the original series only it is not possible to say much about the significance of the postulated relationships. By the ordinary test of the significance of the multiple correlation coefficient R, all but six of the 144 analyses set out in Table 4 appear significant at the 1 per cent level. The exceptional cases are

---

* The symbol 2' stands for the logarithm of money income and the symbol 3/4 stands for the logarithm of the price ratio (p/π).

relationships 35, 85 and 108 (all involving the sets (12) or (12′)) which appear significant only at the 5 per cent level and 14, 56 and 101 (all involving the set (134)) which do not even appear significant at this less exacting level.

TABLE 5. AN ANALYSIS OF THE AVERAGE VALUE OF VON NEUMANN'S RATIO IN DIFFERENT SUBSETS
(AMERICAN DATA)

	Subset					
	(12)	(125)	(134)	(1234)	(1345)	(12345)
1. Number of cases	32	21	16	22	22	12
2. $E(\bar{v})$	2·17	2·17	2·17	2·17	2·17	2·17
3. Actual value of $\bar{v}$	0·97	1·79	1·06	2·16	2·41	2·23
4. (2–3)	1·20	0·38	1·11	0·01	−0·24	−0·06
5. Standard error of (3)	0·10	0·12	0·13	0·11	0·11	0·15

TABLE 6. AN ANALYSIS OF THE DISPERSION OF VON NEUMANN'S RATIO IN DIFFERENT SUBSETS
(AMERICAN DATA)

	Subset		
	(1234)	(1345)	(12345)
1. Number of cases	22	22	12
2. $V(v)$	0·307	0·307	0·307
3. Actual variance computed about $\bar{v}$	0·286	0·276	0·217
4. Actual variance computed about $E(\bar{v})$	0·273	0·321	0·202
5. (2–3)	0·021	0·031	0·090
6. Standard error of (3)	0·087	0·087	0·120

(3) *The Individual Regression Coefficients and their Significance*

An examination of Table 4 shows that in most cases the elasticities are in accordance with theoretical expectations. Unexpected signs appear in analyses 59, 67, 72, 83 and 119; in only one case, 83, are the coefficients with unexpected signs significant.

(a) *Income elasticities.* In the great majority of cases these elasticities are significant and the standard errors are, in many cases, small compared with the corresponding standard errors for the substitution elasticities. There is a tendency where income is introduced for the elasticities in alternative analyses for the same commodity to be similar in magnitude and to be in rough conformity with what might be expected *a priori*. At the same time the differences between alternative estimates are sometimes large compared with the estimated standard errors and in many cases analyses, satisfactory from the standpoint of goodness of fit, are made without income being introduced at all, indicating that a satisfactory fit can be obtained with an income elasticity of zero.

The elasticities for different commodities show a considerable range of variation from the order of one-half for food to two for passenger cars and four for pleasure craft.

(b) *Own-price substitution elasticities.* While these elasticities are almost always negative, the standard errors appear on the whole to be substantially larger than in the case of the income elasticities. There are considerable differences between the estimates in alternative analyses for the same commodities and a wider range of variation between commodities than in the case of the income elasticities. Particularly large values occur where the two price series are alone introduced as determining variables: compare analyses 32, 39, 44, 62, 71, 78, 101, 109, 115 and 128.

(c) *All-other-price substitution elasticities. Mutatis mutandis* the position of these elasticities is similar to those under (b) described in the last paragraph. On the whole they tend, apart from sign, to be somewhat larger than the own-price substitution elasticities. Of the 73 relevant analyses the sum of the two elasticities is positive in 60 cases and negative in 13 cases. Of the 48 analyses out of the above 73 in which the sum appears to be significantly different from zero it is positive in 45 cases and negative in 3 cases.

(d) *Residual trends.* The first impression given by the figures in Table 4 is that the residual trend is of immense importance. A contribution of as much as 5 per cent per annum cumulative up or down is by no means uncommon. Further investigation as summarized in Table 7 indicates that there are considerable differences in the residual trends shown in alternative analyses for the same commodity. In particular the trend coefficients shown in the subset (125) are frequently negative and usually less than those in the subset (1345). This is not surprising since in the two subsets different economic variables as well as specific indicators of changes in tastes, habits, etc., are omitted, so that in the different analyses the residual trends are standing for different sets of omitted influences. On the whole the larger set (12345) shows less extreme values for the residual trend coefficients.

(e) *Other factors.* In the case of passenger car parts and accessories, the number of motor vehicle registrations is introduced as a determining variable. Although the zero order correlation between this variable and the variable to be explained is high, $r_{16} = 0.94$, it appears that in the larger subsets, e.g. (12346) shown in Table 4, the influence of this factor is negative. This seems paradoxical but it may be that the rising stock of motor vehicles was accompanied by increased reliability and a tendency to scrap vehicles at an earlier stage, both factors making for a decreased use of spares, other things being equal, as the stock of vehicles grew.

(4) *How far is the Proportionality Condition Satisfied?*

As already remarked in 3(c) above the all-other-price substitution elasticities tend to be higher than the own-price substitution elasticities.

TABLE 7. RESIDUAL TREND COEFFICIENTS IN DIFFERENT SUBSETS
(AMERICAN DATA)

Commodity	Subset		
	(125)	(1345)	(12345)
Food	...	...	0.003 ± 0.003
Tobacco	0.008 ± 0.002	0.034 ± 0.002	0.021 ± 0.005
Clothing	-0.012 ± 0.005	...	...
Clocks, Watches and Jewelry	-0.047 ± 0.016	0.053 ± 0.007	...
Toilet Preparations and Sundries	...	0.034 ± 0.007	...
House Furniture and Floor Coverings	...	0.062 ± 0.007	-0.007 ± 0.013
Sewing Machines, Washing Machines and Refrigerators	...	0.036 ± 0.016	...
Electrical Appliances	0.060 ± 0.011	0.074 ± 0.018	...
Heating and Cooking Apparatus	-0.035 ± 0.007	...	...
House Furnishings and Equipment	...	0.044 ± 0.005	-0.004 ± 0.013
Tools	-0.028 ± 0.004	0.088 ± 0.017	...
Cleaning and Polishing Preparations	...	0.039 ± 0.005	0.043 ± 0.018
Writing Equipment	-0.058 ± 0.009	(0.048 ± 0.005)	...
Stationery and Writing Supplies	0.016 ± 0.005	0.075 ± 0.004	...
Household Paper Products	0.083 ± 0.008	0.073 ± 0.014	0.041 ± 0.017
Drug Preparations and Household Sundries	0.015 ± 0.003	0.042 ± 0.004	0.036 ± 0.008
Ophthalmic Products, etc.	0.026 ± 0.005	(0.070 ± 0.004)	...
Monuments and Tombstones	-0.057 ± 0.009	0.024 ± 0.006	-0.029 ± 0.018
Passenger Cars	-0.039 ± 0.017	0.138 ± 0.024	...
Tyres and Tubes	-0.081 ± 0.013	...	...
Passenger Car Parts and Accessories	0.026 ± 0.007	...	...
Gasoline and Oil	0.028 ± 0.003	0.049 ± 0.001	0.043 ± 0.003
Luggage	...	0.032 ± 0.006	0.025 ± 0.024
Books and Other Durable Printed Matter	-0.028 ± 0.006	0.022 ± 0.007	...
Magazines, Newspapers and Other Printed Matter	...	(0.030 ± 0.003)	...
Toys, Games and Sports Supplies	-0.013 ± 0.003	0.033 ± 0.007	0.001 ± 0.007
Wheel Goods, Durable Toys, etc.	0.025 ± 0.010	0.080 ± 0.008	...
Pleasure Craft	-0.050 ± 0.011	0.142 ± 0.023	...
Radios	...	0.048 ± 0.024	...
Pianos, and Other Musical Instruments	-0.053 ± 0.014	0.071 ± 0.009	0.047 ± 0.031 (-0.049 ± 0.016)

Note. The values in brackets are derived from analyses in which the proportionality condition is assumed to be satisfied exactly, i.e. from subsets of the form (13/45) or (123/45).

TABLE 8. AN ANALYSIS OF THE PROPORTIONALITY CONDITION IN DIFFERENT SUBSETS
(AMERICAN DATA)

	Subset					
	(134)	(1234)	(1345)	(12345)	(12346)	All subsets
Significant difference	7	14	21	5	1	48
No significant difference	9	8	1	7	0	25
Total	16	22	22	12	1	73

The 73 cases in which the comparison can be made are distributed over different subsets as shown in Table 8.

If it could be assumed that all the 'other' prices varied in proportion these results would suggest a significant departure from rational behaviour on the part of consumers. This assumption cannot, however, be made and it is always possible that the prices of close substitutes and complements did not in any particular case move closely with the index of all other prices. In such cases the short cut adopted here would not be justified and an ardent believer in the rationality of consumers' behaviour could claim that these results show that in many cases it is not.

XXVIII. THE SOURCES USED IN THE AMERICAN ANALYSES

In order to carry out the analyses of the preceding section it was necessary to match price and expenditure series. Most of the expenditure series have been revised from time to time and the latest series have not been used where recalculations did not seem worth while. For these reasons I shall set out in Table 9 the sources of the actual series that have been used.

Apart from information relating to the cost of living index and its weights, all the data used appeared in special articles in the *Survey of Current Business*. The series for disposable income came from the *Survey* for April 1944 and the method of calculation is as set out in an earlier article.* The series for consumers' expenditure came either from the *Survey* for June 1944† or from the *National Income Supplement* to the *Survey* (July 1947).‡ The price series for each group were taken from an article in the *Survey* for May 1943§ and were related to the expenditure series as shown in the following table. The quantity series were obtained by dividing the expenditure series by the corresponding price series. The cost of living index prepared by the Bureau of Labor Statistics‖ was used as an index of all other prices after an allowance, in appropriate cases, for the contribution made by the price movement of the commodity or group in question. In many cases, as shown in Table 9, the appropriate weight of a commodity or group in the index was known¶ but the movement of the indicator was not. In these cases an allowance was made for the price movement of the commodity or group based on the price series used here.

Unfortunately no price series are available for services with the exception of the rent component in the cost of living index. For this

* See 'The Analysis of Market Demand', loc cit. (1945), p. 336.
† See 'Consumption Expenditures 1929–43', by W. H. Shaw, loc. cit. pp. 6–13.
‡ Loc. cit. table 30.
§ See 'Price Deflators for Consumer Commodities and Capital Equipment', by H. Shavell, loc. cit. pp. 13–21.
‖ See, for example, *Statistical Abstract of the United States*, 1943, pp. 404–5.
¶ See *Description of the Cost-of-Living Index of the Bureau of Labor Statistics* (1943).

TABLE 9. SOURCES OF DATA FOR SPECIFIC COMMODITIES USED IN THE ANALYSES OF SECTION XXVII

Commodity	Source of		Weight in cost of living index (%)
	Consumers' expenditure series	Price series	
Food	A, sum of items I. 1 to I. 4 less the value of alcoholic beverages included in these items from footnote 2 on p. 11	C, item 1	35·4
Tobacco	A, item I. 5	C, item 3	2·4
Footwear	A, item II. 1	C, item 15	1·9
Clothing	A, item II. 3	C, items 14, 16 and 17 with weights 93, 2 and 5 respectively	8·4
Clocks, Watches and Jewelry	A, item II. 11	C, items 30 and 31 with weights 40 and 60 respectively	...
Toilet Preparations and Sundries	A, item III. 1	C, item 5	1·2
House Furniture and Floor Coverings	A, items V. 1 and V. 2	C, items 20 and 21 with weights 57·5 and 42·5 respectively	1·8
Sewing Machines, Washing Machines and Refrigerators	A, item V. 3	C, item 24	1·2
Electrical Appliances	A, item V. 4	C, item 25	...
Heating and Cooking Apparatus	A, item V. 6	C, item 23	...
China, Glassware, Tableware, etc.	A, item V. 7	C, item 26	...
House Furnishings and Equipment	A, items V. 8 and V. 9	C, items 17, 18 and 22 with weights 20, 45 and 35 respectively	...
Tools	A, item V. 10	D, item 56	...
Cleaning and Polishing Preparations	B, item V. 16	C, item 6	...
Writing Equipment	B, item V. 9	C, item 33	...
Stationery and Writing Supplies	B, item V. 18	C, item 8	...
Household Paper Products	B, item V. 17	C, item 9	...
Household Fuel	A, items V. 5 and V. 19	C, items 11 and 12 with weights 50 and 50 respectively	3·4
Drug Preparations and Household Medical Sundries	A, item VI. 1	C, item 4	0·8
Ophthalmic Products, etc.	B, item VI. 2	C, item 34	...
Monuments and Tombstones	B, item VI. 18	C, item 35	...
Passenger Cars	A, item VIII. 1a	C, item 38	2·2
Tyres and Tubes	A, item VIII. 1c	C, item 39	...
Passenger Car Parts and Accessories	B, item VIII. 1c	C, item 40	...
Gasoline and Oil	B, item VIII. 1e	C, item 13	2·1
Luggage	A, item VIII. 4	C, item 36	...
Books and Other Durable Printed Matter	A, item IX. 5a	C, item 32	...
Magazines, Newspapers and Other Printed Matter	A, item IX. 5b	C, item 7	1·2
Toys, Games and Sports Supplies	A, item IX. 5d	C, items 10 and 19 with weights 60 and 40 respectively	...
Wheel Goods, Durable Toys, etc.	B, item IX, 5e	C, item 37	...
Pleasure Craft	B, item IX. 5f	C, item 41	...
Radios	B, item IX. 5h	C, item 27	...
Pianos and Other Musical Instruments	A, item IX. 5j	C, items 28 and 29 with weights 65 and 35 respectively	...

Note. The letters A, B, C and D are used to denote the following sources: A: Shaw's article in *S.C.B.* (June 1944), table 2. B: *National Income Supplement* to *S.C.B.* (July 1947), table 30. C: Shavell's article in *S.C.B.* (May 1943), table 1. D: Shavell's article in *S.C.B.* (May 1943), table 3.

reason no services were included in the analyses of the last section. Also the price series used here are not available for the post-war years so that it is impossible to see how closely the demand equations based on pre-war experience reproduce the level and fluctuations of post-war demand.

XXIX. CONCLUDING REMARKS

At the end of this brief survey of the role of measurement in economics I shall attempt some general remarks on the lessons that seem to me to emerge and on a few other matters which arise out of the recent growth of quantitative economics and its use in economic policy. I have tried to illustrate the varied needs for measurement in describing economic situations and processes, in testing theories, in estimating the influence of one factor on another and in prediction. The importance of measurement for all these purposes is now generally recognized and an unprecedented amount of quantitative work is now being done by economists. The eighteenth field of research listed by Newmarch nearly eighty years ago has truly come into its own as a subject of intellectual interest and practical importance.

The past has seen many a battle of giants over the respective merits of the theoretical and empirical approaches to economic problems. There are signs that this false dichotomy is becoming recognized more and more widely for what it is. Only recently 'measurement without theory' has been condemned in high places and if theory without measurement has not come in explicitly for similar treatment the shift of interest as evidenced in the literature leaves the unexpressed views little in doubt. These remarks must not of course be taken as a plea against specialization; obviously a man who is an acknowledged master at conducting economic and social surveys may be no better than a raw hand at constructing theories of international trade or imperfect competition. They are intended only to combat the notion that either theory by itself or empiricism by itself has exclusive charge of the key to useful knowledge. No doubt in some branches of economics what is most urgently needed is a better theoretical formulation, in others a better description of what actually happens. In much of economics, however, there exist tolerable theories and a great many facts which have a bearing on these theories. The great need is to get the specialists in different aspects of a given field to work together, show a reasonable understanding of and respect for one another's disciplines and advance to problems which none could tackle on his own.

Just as unsympathetic specialization is a bar to advance so also is the undue exclusiveness sometimes to be observed in economists. The determination to deal only with the economic aspect of problems doubtless makes for tidy theories and all the pleasures of staying on the home ground. But inasmuch as the economic aspect is only a part of most actual problems its single-minded pursuit leads to distortion and incompleteness. This is particularly so at the present time when social influences are coming again to play a larger part in shaping the changes in society than they did in past eras of modified *laissez-faire* and when in many respects the economic system is maintained as an act of policy in a state in which it can only be kept in equilibrium by forces which must be classed as non-economic. Here again the moral seems to be not less specialization but more co-operation and understanding between economists and those who work in other branches of the social sciences.

Co-operation and understanding are not, however, enough. Economic theory makes use of an elaborate system of concepts linked together by equations of definition some of which have been illustrated in the sections on social accounting. At the same time the practical needs of economic policy require that quantitative expression be given to the empirical correlates of many of these theoretical variables. To do this satisfactorily we have to put greater emphasis than in the past on economic design in the collection of economic statistics. That is to say there is an increasing area of factual knowledge in which it is necessary to collect information which will reflect theoretical variables defined in advance, rather than to rely on the manipulation of existing statistics collected for a narrower administrative purpose. And just as economic design is important in deciding what information shall be collected, so in deciding how to collect this information statistical design is equally important. That is to say the organizations responsible for collecting statistics should endeavour systematically to choose the cheapest method consistent with the nature and degree of reliability of the information required. The fact that much of the new information needed for economic policy does not involve administrative action in individual cases makes it possible to apply sampling methods more freely than could be contemplated with much of the older type of administrative statistical information.

New administrative needs calling for regular estimates of national income, asset formation, saving and the like and for predictions of all these variables have led in recent years to a greater emphasis on estimation as opposed to recording and tabulation in official statistics. This development is greatly to be welcomed and will certainly continue. At the moment, however, when the necessary information on which to base the estimates is incomplete and when their reliability can at best be roughly assessed, it is a question how far the statistician or economist should go in meeting the demand for estimates when there is very little factual material available. On the positive side it may be said that it is better that policy should be framed with some idea, even if only a vague one, of the orders of magnitude involved than with no idea at all. Against this it may be argued that too great a willingness to give answers to questions that cannot be answered debases the statistical coinage. Orders of magnitude, based not on fact but on hopes and prejudices, may receive undue attention because they are put forward by specialists who are supposed to be concerned solely with facts or rational deductions from fact. As a consequence the layman may become confused on the line between fact and speculation.

The ethical problem which this situation poses to the investigator is certainly a difficult one, but like other ethical problems requires that some weight be attached to the probable consequences of following different lines of action. From the point of view of the scholar there cannot be much to be gained from attempting to draw conclusions from observations so insecure that conflicting results would follow if some of the variables were changed within their supposed margins of error. From the point of view of the economic adviser on the other hand the position is different because as a rule he is not in a position to decide the areas of activity in which decisions are to be taken and so must do his best with problems that are set to him and not just with those of his own choosing. To some extent he may be able to influence the general way in which problems of policy are formulated, but it is hardly possible that he can greatly influence the sort of information that is called for. In such circumstances he cannot be expected to remain silent simply because his scientific conscience is continually shocked at the guesswork involved in producing answers. An expert adviser is no doubt at fault if he fails to give any indication of what he believes to be the margins of error of his estimates and to point out the consequences for policy of uncertainties in the factual basis of his conclusions. But unless this is very skilfully done the net effect of his attempts may simply be to discredit his point of view because he, though an expert, is uncertain like everyone else and moreover expresses his uncertainty in a particularly baffling manner. Responsibility for this state of affairs lies not with expert advisers but with the general system of education which even nowadays relegates probability and uncertain inference to a narrow specialism when in its elements at any rate it should form part of the training of everyone.

In conclusion I shall consider the issue of fundamental problems *versus* questions of the day as subjects of research. Obviously at the present time there are innumerable practical problems urgently in need of examination. It might be argued that their solution should take precedence over both methodological investigations, designed to show how to collect information, how to test hypotheses or how to make predictions more efficiently, and the attendant theoretical inquiries which all of these involve. Such a view would, in my opinion, be wholly mistaken, and this for two main reasons. In the first place while there is certainly scope for research at the descriptive level and into the probable outcome of existing trends, neither the resources nor the knowledge available to research workers in the universities and private research institutes is sufficient as a rule to enable them to make an effective contribution to the solution of day to day problems of policy. In the second place many of these problems can only be satisfactorily resolved by methodological research; indeed such research is unavoidable if general agreement is to be reached on many practical issues. For example it is of practical importance to be able to compare the national accounts of different countries. To do this it is necessary to put the information for the countries to be compared into a common framework. While any one country concerned may be satisfied with the framework it in fact uses, agreement can only be reached on the basis of principles and conventions which are generally acceptable, so that for a purely practical purpose questions of definition and measurement have to be reopened and discussed. Again many practical issues, such as the usefulness of currency devaluation or the implications of removing rationing, depend among other things on the value of certain demand and supply elasticities. While action has to be taken in the absence of any reliable information about these values it is clear that similar problems will arise again and that it will be helpful if in the meantime fundamental research has shown how such values may be determined to the necessary degree of accuracy.

Printed in the United States
By Bookmasters